THE
ENCHANTED BAY

Patrick J. Mahoney, or Pádraig Fhia Ó Mathúna, is an award-winning historian and writer. He is currently a Government of Ireland Postdoctoral Fellow at the University of Galway. Between 2021 and 2023, he was a researcher on the Harvard-based Fionn Folklore Database. A former Fulbright scholar, his publications include a critical volume of the translated works of Irish language writer Eoin Ua Cathail, entitled *Recovering an Irish Voice from the American Frontier* (2021).

Cormac K.H. O'Malley was born in Ireland, moved to the USA in 1957, studied history at Harvard and law at Columbia, and enjoyed a successful thirty-year international legal career. In retirement, he has pursued research on modern Irish history and the legacy of his parents, Ernie O'Malley and artist Helen Hooker O'Malley. He has lectured broadly on his family legacy and Irish history.

THE
ENCHANTED BAY

Tales and Legends from Ernie O'Malley's
Irish Folklore Collection

Edited by
Cormac K.H. O'Malley and Patrick J. Mahoney

Photographs by
Helen Hooker O'Malley

Illustrations by
Paula McGloin

MERRION
PRESS

First published in 2024 by
Merrion Press
10 George's Street
Newbridge
Co. Kildare
Ireland
www.merrionpress.ie

© Cormac O'Malley, 2024

9781785375286 (Hardback)
9781785375347 (eBook)

A CIP catalogue record for this book is
available from the British Library.

Typeset in Calluna 11.5/17 pt

Cover design by Paula McGloin
Maps by Rainer Kosbi

Merrion Press is a member of Publishing Ireland

This first volume of tales and legends from Clew Bay is dedicated to Sean Cadden of Westport, Michael Mulchrone of Castlebar and Peter Mullowney of Newport. Without their insight, dedication, knowledge of local lore, surnames, townlands, Mayo geography and history, this work would never have been put in publishable form.

Contents

৴৶৽

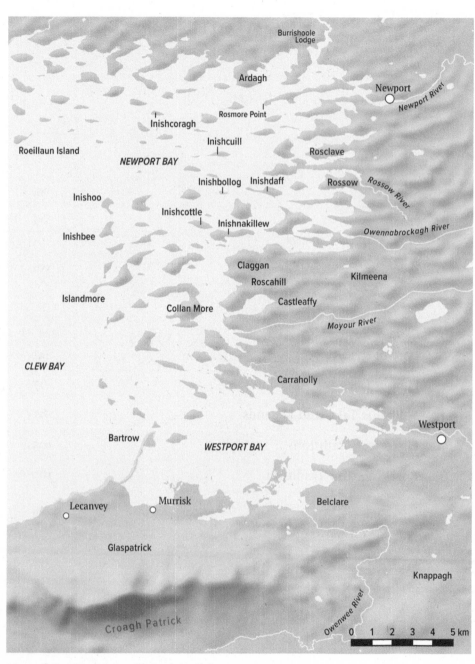

Map of County Mayo. (Rainer Kosbi)

Map of Clew Bay, County Mayo. (Rainer Kosbi)

Map of South West Mayo, Louisburgh to Killary Harbour. (Rainer Kosbi)

Ernie O'Malley at wedge tomb, Louisburgh, Co. Mayo, 1938.

Preface

EADERS OF THIS REMARKABLE COLLECTION of oral literature will perhaps be surprised that it should come from the pen of a revolutionary and chronicler of Ireland's War of Independence struggles. But Ernie O'Malley was imbued from his childhood with the wonders of storytelling; and it stirred his imagination and left him alert in his adulthood to oral tradition.

He was by instinct a folklore collector - even during the difficult revolutionary years he was fascinated by local tales and legends - and on his return to Ireland in the 1930s he would have been receptive to the scholarly interest of the time in recording and studying folklore. In Dublin, he and his wife, Helen, mixed with artists and intellectuals, among them Séamus Ó Duilearga, Director of the Irish Folklore Commission, founded in 1935.

His work in the Clew Bay region (1939–42) adds significantly to the folklore footprint of the county, and deepens our understanding of the impact of linguistic change on the oral tradition. This collection complements the documentation by several fine collectors working in the Irish language in the Mayo–Galway area at the time, including Pádraig Ó Moghráin in Achill, Ciarán Bairéad in Louisburgh and Brian Mac Lochlainn in Clifden.

Compelling and highly realistic, the legends told in *The Enchanted Bay* are often closely linked to people and places. They are especially rich in terms of supernatural lore – an area of oral tradition in which O'Malley took an active interest. The abundance of fairy legends testifies to the strength of this aspect of folk belief at that time. In many of the tales, fairies play a key role, indicating their perceived mastery over land and sea. Often they are depicted competing with or threatening fishermen, but there are profitable exchanges in these encounters too – the gift of fish to a fairy boat crew is rewarded with special knowledge of where to fish, and there are striking accounts of phantom boats appearing to warn fishermen of a pending storm. Maritime lore is an exceptionally rich thread running through the book. Some accounts are historical in nature, recalling drownings and shipwrecks, including poignant stories of drowned fishermen returning from the dead to warn or assist boatmen in difficulty.

Historical events and figures also feature strongly, including local traditions of landlords such as Major Bingham and Sir Samuel O'Malley, who are often depicted against the backdrop of evictions and land agitation. Accounts of uprisings – ranging from Cromwell's time to 1798, and the later Fenian uprisings – sit alongside stories of the exploits of remarkable men and women, outlaws and faction fights.

A number of the stories are 'memorates', first-hand accounts of supernatural experiences – a genre of folk legend that is comparatively rare in the folklore record. There are also migratory legends. These are stylised narratives with distinctive plots, adapted to local settings. They include the international legend *Midwife to the Fairies* ('The Midwife and the Fairy Child' on page 24 in which a human midwife is called to deliver a fairy child, and *The Milk-Stealing Hare* ('The Hare That Became an Old Woman', page 27), in which a witch takes the form of a hare in order to suck a farmer's cow dry.

The bulk of the stories focus on local tradition and belief but O'Malley also recorded stories with more universal appeal – the highly amusing cycle of tales dealing with the Gobán Saor, the master builder of Irish mythology, and very touching religious tales and legends. This latter genre of oral literature was once extremely popular in Ireland, dealing as it does with important social concepts such as justice, equality and morality.

Ernie O'Malley's contribution to Irish folklore studies is significant. It serves as a fascinating and instructive backdrop to his later monumental task of recording the testimonies of his former military comrades. The skills and methods honed in the course of his folklore collecting, and his grasp and appreciation of memory and the inherent processes of oral transmission, were to stand him in good stead for the ambitious recording project he later undertook.

Dr Críostóir Mac Cárthaigh

Ernie O'Malley listening to a tale, Kilvarnet, Achill Island, Co. Mayo, 1939.

Reflections on Ernie O'Malley and His Tales

❧

MY FATHER, ERNIE O'MALLEY, ONCE had his future told by an old fortune teller who informed him that fighting and trouble lay ahead. Her prediction came true, whether he believed it or not at the time. She may have just being telling a tall tale, but there's no denying the profound impact storytelling had on my father from an early age. His first memoir, *On Another Man's Wound*, begins with the words: 'Our nurse, Nannie, told my eldest brother and me stories and legends. Her stories began: "Once upon a time and a very good time it was," and ended with, "They put on the kettle and made tay, and if they weren't happy that you may."'[1] His Nannie, Mary Ann Jordan, was from outside Castlebar, and knew the tales and legends from the countryside. She told them to the children of my staid, conservative, strict, Catholic grandparents, Luke and Marion Malley, who lived on the main street in Castlebar.

These extraordinary tales included legends of the ancient kings of Ireland, the mighty Fionn mac Cumhaill, Ferdia of Connaught who was killed by Cúchulainn of Ulster, the Tuatha Dé Danann and local Mayo proverbs. These legends ignited a lifelong passion, and my father later developed a remarkable understanding not only of Mayo lore, but of Icelandic and Norwegian tales, and of legends in general. As he travelled around Ireland as an Irish Republican Army (IRA) organiser, he would hear of the local legends – the Black Pig's Dyke in Strokestown[2] – or have rural experiences in Dungloe, County Donegal that scared even him.[3]

In the spring of 1919 he was out on Inis Óir organising an IRA company. When it came his turn to tell a tale, he told them of 'Till Eulenspiegel, some of Hakluyt's sea tales, Bricriu's Feast and the Story of Burnt Njal … and the story of Mac Datho's Boar'.[4]

While in prison for twenty months during the Irish Civil War, he read extensively, including European myths and legends. When he met the Irish folklorist, Ella Young, in New Mexico in 1929, they spoke of the need to preserve Irish folklore and ballads.[5] While he was in New Mexico and Mexico (in 1931), he visited several pueblos and was interested in the indigenous arts, cultures and tales, and recorded in his diaries what he heard and saw. He knew the American folklorist, Frances Toor, who wrote extensively on Mexican customs, myths and folkways. His library contains over twenty-five books on folklore, including Mexican and British folklore journals and Kuno Meyer's books.

In the US in 1934, after completing his two memoirs, he began writing short fictional vignettes about military incidents during the War of Independence and Civil War that also included Irish folk stories such as 'Maire Cain', 'Michael Óg O'Malley', and 'Sheila, Sean and the Fairies' (unpublished).[6]

When he married my American mother, the artist Helen Hooker, in 1935, they returned to Dublin, where he settled back into the life of an Irish medical student. On their weekends and in the summers, they started a four-year odyssey to photograph and record many of Ireland's major and minor archaeological sites as well as the early and medieval ruined monasteries. My mother was captivated by the Irish countryside, with its bogs, mountains, cottages and rural life and customs in general. She captured these elements in her sensitive images.

During this time, he met folklorist, James Delargy (Séamus Ó Duilearga). His growing interest in the traditional expression of Ireland's culture is evident in his notebooks, in particular. His extensive notes on Irish literature, folklore, poetry, songs and ballads (New York Public Library, 1928–34 and National Library of Ireland, 1936–38).[7] *On Another Man's Wound* includes thirty-two Irish songs and ballads collected during this time.

When my parents moved to Louisburgh, County Mayo in 1938, and later settled in their permanent home in Burrishoole Lodge, near Newport, they continued their photographic project. My mother's photos complement the collection of stories, offering another medium for capturing the social history of the time and place. Her striking photos feature the beauty of Clew Bay's landscape and give an additional layer of insight into the local physical and cultural environment in which she found herself living. My father had a passion for sailing solo in Clew Bay, and he got to know some of the Clew Bay islanders, such as Patrick Quinn, Inishcottle, and Josie Gill, Islandmore, who often visited at Burrishoole Lodge. His notebooks (summer 1939) contain numerous notes on Clew Bay islands: their stories and local anecdotes, animals, tides, fishing, types of fish, fair days and patterns.[8]

In the winter of 1940 he began writing down tales he heard from locals on the islands and mainland, and he continued in early

1942. No doubt, one informant recommended another, and he took down over 330 tales from at least nineteen men and two women. He recorded these stories in a notebook late at night, sitting by a fireplace, probably with a glass in his hand. His handwriting was extremely poor, almost illegible. Some tales were rewritten a little while later. There were many errors in his writing because he wrote what he heard phonetically and did not know the Irish language well nor know the spellings of local family names, townlands or islands. The sad thing is that he never revisited his notebooks to prepare them for publication. They lay untouched for forty years, until I discovered one of them in 1981.

When he returned to live part-time in Dublin in 1944, he switched his focus from folk tales to writing articles as an art critic. In 1947 he became the books editor for the *Bell* and immersed himself in the Dublin literary world. During this time, he commenced another project, interviewing 450 comrades from the War of Independence and Civil War. This work included handwritten ballads and songs. In many ways, these military interviews were a continuation of his earlier folk tale project. No doubt, for him, all these elements represented the background to the centuries of struggle for Irish independence. During this literary period, he started to write fiction again.

I had no idea my father was interested in folk tales until I started to edit these tales he had collected before I was born. But I recognised two of them, 'The Flax Threshers Under the Sea' (see p. 50) and 'The Man Who Caught the Mermaid' (see p. 52), which means he probably told them to me. The latter one inspired his short story 'The Dark Girl', as yet unpublished.[9]

Recapturing old Ireland and expressing the ancient spirit of the Irish culture through stories were part of my father's lifelong ambition. I hope that creating this collection of stories in *The Enchanted Bay: Tales and Legends from Ernie O'Malley's Irish Folklore Collection* goes some way towards realising his ambition and capturing this ancient spirit.

Cormac K.H. O'Malley

Mermaid, Clonfert Cathedral, Co. Galway, 1939.

CHAPTER 1

Tales of the Supernatural

⟡

The Loughraman's Three Wishes

THERE WAS A POOR COUPLE, who had been evicted, and they lived near Louisburgh on a poor bit of bog. They had only one cow and three or four garsúns. They found it hard to make ends meet, and they were always wishing for money and hoping to be rich expecting a legacy or if possible to catch a Loughraman because it was well known that the Loughraman's has money hid.

One morning early the ould man of the house saw this little maneen and caught him. He asked him where he kept his money, but he said he had none. The ould man wouldn't believe him and squeezed him as if he would choke him. Again, the Loughraman said he had none and then he squealed and begged for his life. The ould man wouldn't let him go but kept hold of him by the neck until he brought him home to his wife. Still the ould man kept demanding the money and threatening him and the poor little fellow was continuing to make excuses. Finally, he said if they'd let him go as he had no money, he'd give them what 'id be as good to the pair of them, three wishes, whatever they'd wish for, any three things, and he'd grant it to them, but only if they let him go.

The ould man and his wife were quite satisfied with his promise and gave him his liberty. They knew he wouldn't tell a lie. They consulted between themselves on what to do. They arranged to change their dwelling if they got plenty of money and to get a big house and farm with plenty of land and stock and then reserve the third wish 'til they'd be settled down in their new home.

To start their plans and operations for their new lives, they took their one little cow to the next market day in the nearby town and sold her cheap to the first bidder for only £5.10. The buyer and the man of the house went in to the local pub, as is the custom after a sale, to drink the luck money while the woman remained with the cow 'til they'd come out. She began talking to another woman, and as they were talking, a man passed by then with three beautiful curly beets for sale, and when she saw the beets, she said to the other woman,

'I wish I had one of them beets.' Immediately, to her surprise and shock, it was shoved under her arm. She was so startled, she went in to her husband and told him what had happened.

'Oh,' she says, 'don't kill me when you hear what I've done,' and she rattled on.

'What have you done at all? What's the matter with you?' says he.

'Oh. I saw a man on the street with three nice curly beets, and I said to him, "I wish I had one of them beets," and as soon as I had the words out of my mouth, the beets was shoved under me arm, and then I knew what I had done.'

Now, the husband on hearing this misuse of one of the three wishes became excited and says, 'I wish it was up your arse, it was stuck.'

While they were speaking, the beet straight away went up the wife's arse. They were both in a hard fix then. She was roaring with pain, and he knew he also had made a mistake. The only remedy remained a third wish to have the beet come down again. After that they both went home just as poor as ever. But it is thought that if he hadn't threatened the Loughraman in the first place, and if he had asked him decently for the money, your little man wouldn't have played such a trick on him.[1]

Domhnall a Pooca

One evening when Daniel was a young man and his mother was still alive, he went walking down on the dooagh or machair, that flat sandy grassland that runs along the edge of the sea. It was late in the evening and didn't he come across a fine-looking woman walking alone along the dooagh, and she seemed to have gone astray. He greeted her, but she didn't respond. She was a well-dressed woman, better than anyone around Louisburgh at the time. He didn't know what to do with her, and so he brought her to the house. On the way there, she didn't speak a word. It was late when they got there, and she went right to bed. When he got up the next morning, he went to greet her and found her clothes were there all laid out neatly, but there was no sign of her. She had gone.

At about the same time, it was rumoured that a woman had gone missing in Achill. They never found out who she was.

After that Daniel was always called Domhnall a Pooca (of the ghost). He got married afterwards to a sister of Doctor Burke, and they had children, and some of them emigrated to America and are in America still. One of his descendants was Father Leo Richard Ward, a priest in the University of Notre Dame in Indiana, and he came back to Louisburgh looking for Daniel's relations. He wrote the book *God in an Irish Kitchen*. There were Morrisons over there who were also said to be relatives of his.[2]

The Fairy Wind That Cried Dónall, Dónall

When I was a young lad, about two and a half years, there was a man who lived down below me in Inishnakillew, and his name was Dónall Máille. One day, he was digging potatoes in the harvest time, and he came round a corner of his field with his basket full of potatoes between his hands. The wind suddenly caught him and lifted him over the wall and abused him. When he landed he was bleeding all over, and he came in here to the house, still with a basket of new potatoes between his hands.

'What a wind, Nelly, what a wind,' he says to me mother. 'Nelly,' he says, 'that's an awful whirlwind that lifted me across the ditches and look it has near all destroyed me elbow where I fell against the ditch.'

'Oh, damn it,' says Nelly, 'it won't be worth a pin.'

Me grandmother and a neighbour's girl, Jack John Quinn's aunt, was over beyond on that long hill on Inishnakillew minding cattle, and as that sudden storm passed over, didn't they hear a sound all around them 'Dónall, Dónall, Dónall.'

Dónall recovered, but on the next Saint Martin's Day evening, the 11th of November, he was drownded at Newport Quay, and though he was seventy-four, he was a man who could swim from Inishnakillew to Inishoo.

Some wild winds come up suddenly and bounce off the cliffs, and they're very dangerous, and if one has a sail up, one could hear them whistling, but it's best to haul one's sails down for if one does, they'll stay away and not touch the boat.

When you hear a man's name crying out going in the wind, there's something wrong. None of us said anything about hearing the voice 'til poor Dónall was drownded. Only then did we talk about hearing his name being called by the passing wind.

Dónall married but went out to America and left his family here in Inishnakillew. Two years before he drownded, he came home.[3]

***

The Stone That Came Back

There was a young man, Hildebrand, the son of an agent of Lord Lucan. Once he was out in Inishturk on business and decided to go on over to Caher Island, which is not far away. On the little gable on St Patrick's bed, there was a good-sized stone laying there.

Hildebrand went in and took that stone away with him. The stone was as light as a feather. He took it and pitched it in to the deepest spot of the sea to the west of Caher. The stone bubbled away and went to the bottom of the sea, as would any stone. Now, when Hildebrand went by St Patrick's bed a little later, wasn't the stone back in its usual place on the little gable.

Shortly thereafter young Hildebrand was back on the mainland and going along this road by a little lake, and he was somehow moved to walk out in to the lake, and it was five foot deep. A man seeing him said, 'You got the same ducking yourself as good as you gave the stone.' He didn't bother again about the stone, but he hung down his head.

There are a lot of clean looking stones, and if a stone is turned up, you'd never find any insects under it, not even the slightest sight of a living thing creeping under them.[4]

The Spirit Lover and the Blacksmith

Once upon a time there was a young girl who lived in the parish of Louisburgh, and she was in love with a young man, but sadly, he died suddenly. She was distraught but resigned to her fate, but her lover's spirit returned to visit her and tried to take her away.

The young lover who died came back in the form of a man, and he tried to take his girl away. The man was the spirit of her lover. He came in to her house and carried her off with him, and she was riding behind him on his horse.

Now, there was something amiss with the horse's shoe, and so when the man saw a forge in the next village, he decided to stop by the forge to have the shoe fixed. The blacksmith was working, but he stopped as the rider wanted the smith to attend to him right away. While the smith was working away on the shoe, didn't he get a sense that there was something strange going on between the rider and the girl. So didn't he fling a hot iron horseshoe at the rider and at the same time, he grabbed the girl. He pulled her off the horse. The two of them fought over the girl. The rider caught a hold of the girl by the thigh and pulled off pieces of her flesh.[5]

☙

The Graveyard That Moved

Once there was a strip of land that used to extend out to sea not too far from Killeen for about half a mile by a mound, but the parish decided to start a new graveyard inland about one and a half miles straight up towards the hills. Now, there was a flag stone over a grave there, and they got that flag from a slate quarry in Feenune, just below Louisburgh.

One morning when the people woke up and looked outside, they saw that the newly built graveyard had been lifted totally back down to where the old one was down on the strand by the mound, and ever after that the people went down and buried their dead there. It was said that the new graveyard had been located in a place which interrupted the comings and goings of the fairies there.[6]

The Phantom Army Fights

One fine spring day there was a station being held in a house in the village of Carrowmore, near Louisburgh. After the confession, the people came outside the house which stood on a rise looking south out across towards the Sheeffry Hills. The people could see that a full-scale battle was going on just about a mile and a half away. There were cavalry and footmen charging each other near Aughteenaveen in Furmoyle. The people were looking at the battle for a good while, and more people came out of the house to look on when they heard of the excitement. It was brought to the priest's attention, and even he came out to watch the skirmish. They were all out looking at it for a good while, and then the battle disappeared suddenly.[7]

The Multitude of Little Men

Me father-in-law went in to Omey Island where he had a holding of land to see his cattle late one day. It is partially a sandy land there. The grass of that island is very good for cattle, and people use the island for summer grazing. It saves them bringing in bran to feed them, and it cures the dreaded crupá when there's a phosphorus deficiency. When cattle have crupá, it means the cattle will eat anything like clothes, sticks, old shoes and even the tail of your coat.

Now when your man was returning home across the strand from Omey that evening, he met a whole multitude of small men about three foot high, and he approached them. They gathered round him in a hesitating but curious manner. He knew that he was in a tight corner and wondered what he should do. There were no houses nearby for him to get help, and in any case given the late hour, they would have gone to bed. However, he had his long hook in his hand as he used it to sort out the cattle. He started to swing the hook all around him and told them to clear the way for him. As he moved forward across the strand, they gave way before him, and he passed through them and came home safely.[8]

⟞⟍

Peter Brown and the Spinning Wheel

One day Peter Brown of Derryheeagh, meaning a place with a growth of oak, in Cregganbaun, near Glenkeen, was sent out by his wife to pick up a spinning wheel his wife had loaned to a neighbouring woman. On his way back to his house at a late hour, he heard the hooves of a horse on the road. He guessed it would be his neighbour from Cregganbaun who had gone in to Westport that day. Peter got down in to the bog as he didn't want to be an obstacle on the road in the dark with him carrying the big spinning wheel, and he didn't want to startle his neighbour's horse. While he was waiting below in the bog for him to pass by, he set up his spinning wheel and began to spin. The neighbour was riding along on this bright night, and he cast his eye in on the bog and saw the ghost of a man inside in the bog, and he was spinning. The neighbour on his horse got so frightened that he had by mischance struck the poor man off the road, and so off home with him he went without looking any further.

When Peter finally reached his home, the wife had some very bad news for him – that their neighbour was calling for the priest and doctor because he had seen a ghost down the road. Peter knew well that he was the ghost his neighbour had seen, and he told the whole story to his wife. She told him he had to go at once to his neighbour's house and tell the people there who the ghost really was. Peter went over to the neighbour's house and explained the whole matter and told them not to bother sending for the priest and doctor. Now the neighbour was still so frightened by the sight of the ghost that he wouldn't believe Peter at all and insisted on calling the priest and doctor to cure him of his ailment which had led him to seeing the ghost. After some time, the neighbour man calmed down and came back to his senses, and everything was alright then.[9]

The King of Leinster's Daughter

Port Dún is a fairy fort on the west side of Inishturk near Ballyheer. The family of Diarmuid O'Toole and his family used to live not too far from the fort. It was often thought on Inishturk that he was a half-foolish kind of a fellow anyway. One New Year's night, Diarmuid said to his mother that he was going to see if there was anything going on at the fairy fort, and so he went on out by himself in that direction. When he came to the Dún, he saw three men were coming up from the sea carrying a coffin. He went on over to help them to carry the coffin, and they fled away leaving the coffin. Now he was quite curious as to what might be in it. He put his ear to the coffin and felt the breathing of a living person in the coffin, and so he broke open the lid of the coffin. Didn't he find the most beautiful young lady that could be lying there with jewelries and rings and everything else on her. She was quite a sight. She didn't reply a word to his questions. He took her back to his place and showed her to his mother. She never spoke a word to him. He kept her as his wife for twelve months, and all appeared to be going well.

Now, when the next New Year's night came along, he said to his mother that he'd go to Port Dún again to seek his fortune.

'Yes,' she says, 'and you'll bring another fairy home with you like the last one you brought.'

Her words didn't bother him or stop him, and he went back to the fort. This time he found an entrance, and it ran in under the fort for a quarter of a mile. He edged his way in bit by bit and went as far as he could. Suddenly, he heard some voices and put his ear to a sort of a door he found.

'This night twelve months,' says a voice inside, 'Diarmuid O'Toole took the daughter of the King of Leinster with him.'

'He has had no great satisfaction with her,' says another voice. 'She never spoke a word to him in the twelve months.'

'She wouldn't be so quiet,' says another voice, 'if he took the sleeping pin that's behind in the back of her hair out of it.'

Diarmuid returned home to his house, and when he came in, the mother asked him, 'What news?' and he says, 'Awful good news I bring, mother.'

He called the woman to him, took the sleeping pin out of the back of her hair. She got surprised and asked where she was, and this was her first time talking in twelve months. He told her straight away what had happened, and how he had found her. She lived very contentedly with him until the following summer. Then, she asked him to prepare himself to take a boat and to travel as far as her home in the King of Leinster's house.

When the time came Diarmuid got ready for the long trip and was dressed in his usual old frieze costume. He was a handsome looking man. Now, they journeyed on together and finally came to her home in Leinster. When they came to the king's palace, they knocked on the door and an usher came out. He wouldn't allow them in without acquainting the king. The usher went to the king and says, 'There's a couple at the door, a man in frieze apparel, and the most beautiful looking lady that could be, but just like the princess that was dead, and I'd say it was herself that was there.' The usher came back down and said there was no room for them there. She took the ring off her finger and gave it to the usher to bring up to the king. The minute the king saw the ring, he knew that the woman was his missing dead daughter. They were both received with great rejoicing by the king and his family, and they stayed there then for a time before returning to Inishturk.

There was a second daughter of the king, and she said she wanted to visit her sister in Inishturk, and so she took off to follow them a few months after. When she arrived in Inishturk, she greatly enjoyed the place, and she settled down and got married there.

Now, there are two families in Inishturk that claim the privilege of having a mark, and squint on their eyes as their mark, and they are the descendants of the two sisters who were the daughters of the King of Leinster.[10]

ꙮ

The Woman Taken by the Fairies

There once was a woman living out in Louisburgh on the back of a hill in Aghany near Roonah. These were hard times after the Famine, and she was used to eating and living on shellfish. She was out as usual one afternoon and went down on the seashore where she was picking up some shellfish and edible seaweed or creathnach. The night came on, and she hadn't returned. She went missing. The second day came and went, and she didn't return.

Now, there was a fairy fort near the site of the Aghany school. A neighbouring man, by the name of Gibbons, was helping in the search for the woman. He passed by the fort and shouted at the top of his voice for them to let out the lost woman, mentioning her by her name, that they had in there.

Not too long after that the woman was seen leaving the fort and coming on back by the shore to where she had left her basket of shellfish and seaweed on the ridge of the bank. She picked it up and took it on 'til she came on home. The house was crowded in, of course, as many people from the villages around had gathered to find out any news of the missing woman. The house was thronged. The woman went up to sit by the fireside. Me old grandmother, Kathy Lavelle, came in the door, but the house was so crowded, she couldn't see the woman sitting by the hearth. The woman was relating all she had seen and heard about the people in the fairy fort. Now, one of the fairy people had told her not to eat any food nor take any drink when she got home. Then, didn't the woman shout at the top of her voice to me grandmother asking her to go down and bring her a noggin of buttermilk that she was after drawing in the churn. She went down and brought the noggin of buttermilk back and gave it to her. She drank it, and after that no one ever heard the woman open her mouth again about what happened in the fort or anything else for that matter.[11]

The Fairy Man Who Lent the Seed

There was an ould man who lived on the other side of the hill in Glenkeen, and he had this field of land that was dry but ready for sowing, but the poor fellow had no seed to sow in it. Wasn't he wandering up and down all through the field and him near crying that he hadn't any seed to sow for his field of land. Just then, a smallish man appeared from nowhere, walked up to him at the end of the field.

'Poor man, what's the matter with you?' says he.

'There is something terrible the matter with me. I have no seed to sow my field with and shake it in this field of fine soil,' says the ould man.

'Bad enough, poor man,' says he, 'and what would you give to the man that will find seed for you?'

14

'I don't know what'll I give him,' says he.

'Will you give him half the corn when it's ripe?' asks he.

'I will,' says he, 'and welcome.'

Within three minutes, there was a sack of corn in the field and a man harrowing it. As soon as he did, the small man hurried away and left the corn at the Mercy of God for yielding for him 'til harvest.

When the harvest time came, the field got ripe and ready for cutting, and it was the finest field the ould man ever did see on the side of a hill. He had made a bargain not to touch the corn until he'd call the man. He remembered what the little man had said, 'When the corn is ripe call for me.'

'What'll I call you?' says the ould man.

'My name goes by Scallóg Derrymalley,' says the small man.

When the field was just ripe, didn't the ould man walk one day in to the end of the field. He wanted the price of a hundred weight of oats, and he said he'd cut a few parts of it and thresh it, and he forgot to call for Scallóg. He cut them 'til he threshed a hundred weight of oats and got eight or nine shillings for them. The next day, he landed in the field, and who should land up to him but Scallóg.

'What did you do?' says Scallóg. 'Why didn't you call for me?'

'I got hard up, sir,' says the man, 'and what are going to do now with me,' he says. 'What do you want?' he says.

'All I want,' says Scallóg, 'is the full of me rope,' and the rope was wound about his body. The rope was stretched out fitting in the staves of corn in it, and when he had finished, there wasn't a stave left in the field, but he had them all in the rope, and when he had the rope filled and squeezed, all he says was, 'See if ye can size it on me,' and when the man went poking under the rope, he couldn't move it. Scallóg took it with him on his back and sailed off out on the water with the rope of oats on him. The ould man never seen him again nor any stave of the oats.

The place where the field was located is in a little valley with caves in it, called Scallóg Derrymalley.[12]

⌒

Seán Mhaire Joins the Fairies

Seán Mhaire was a small time farmer who lived out the road from the town with his wife and family. One day he took off to go in to the market in the town, and he had a sack of corn loaded on his donkey cart. When he had finished selling the corn and having one for the road, he started his homeward journey. Now, before he reached home, he was sitting up in the cart, and died there just before reaching his own house. The family took the body in, waked him and then buried him.

The next thing, Seán was hoisted over by the fairies to London and brought to a fine gentleman's big place. The password or byword to get in to the mansion was: 'Hats go round three times, go round – Dublin, Galway and Mayo.' Seán went around the house for a while looking at this and that and then tried to get back in the large room where he had been, but he forgot to say the password. He was left behind in the lurch when all the others took off. It didn't bother him too much, and so he went to sleep.

The next morning everyone got up, they found Seán tucked alone in the room. They searched him for the jewels and bracelets, but they couldn't find them on him. They were all gone. When asked he said he didn't know anything about the jewels and bracelets, but they kept asking him about who had robbed him of them and how. They searched him thoroughly, and he hadn't a thing. He bowed his head and couldn't say anything. Seán was in a difficult position because of the password and was going to be tried and sentenced by the court. Suddenly he heard a voice saying, 'Hats go round,' and immediately afterwards and much to everyone's surprise, didn't he shout out the words of the round. From there he was let go out of the court, and the fine mansion, and he landed back in near his home in Ireland.

Now, it was four weeks since Seán had died and was buried. When he came to his home, it was night time, and he knocked on the door. The wife looked out to see who it was and wouldn't open the door to let him in. She thought it was his ghost. Since he couldn't get in the house, he had to go round to the pig sty and sleep with the pig.

That next day, the wife was going to be married to the priest's boy. The pig was going to pay for the marriage and was to be landed up to the priest to be killed for the feasting. The boy was sent round the first thing in the morning for to fetch the pig and to land him to the priest. When the boy came to the pig house and went to the sty, the next thing he seen was Seán putting his head out from under the straw, and off with the boy – the wind wouldn't overtake him nearly.

'Oh, Lord, Father,' the boy says to the priest, 'isn't Seán within in the sty with the pig?'

It was Sunday, and the people were all going to Mass so Seán went up to his own door, and didn't his eldest son come out and recognise him.

'Oh. Where were you, father?' asks the son.

'Where's your mother?' asks Seán.

'She's gone off to Mass,' says the son.

'Well then, I'll best go too,' says Seán, and he sets off for Mass. Many of the neighbours were already on the road headed to Mass. All that was on the road before him, as soon as they looked back and seen Seán, it was off with them as fast as they could go.

There was a woman carrying another lame woman on the road. When she looked behind her, didn't she see Seán, and she threw down the lame woman and left her to her fate. When he was drawing very near the lame woman, she raised herself three times off the ground and when she saw him coming, she too suddenly took off hobbling all the way but fast like.

Seán got to the chapel and made his way in. Then suddenly every door that was in the chapel couldn't hardly hold the people as they were rushing out in such a hurry. Seán was left there with the priest, and the priest was quite timorous, and he left too. Seán had plenty of time to say his prayers. There wasn't a person to disturb him in the church. After that Seán landed back home to Nancy, and Nancy began to look at him in an inquiring way.

He up and says to Nancy, 'What's the matter with you at all?'

'Oh. Seán, oh,' says she, 'aren't you four weeks dead?'

He told her what happened to him – that he had been taken to London, had got the best food to eat and wines in the cellars to drink from the big house, and they treated him well, and they had to have a human with them. He told her the whole story, and everything was fine again after that.[13]

The Devil's Coach-Horse Beetle

Once in the area around Ballina there was a wandering labourer or a spailpín who moved from place to place working at various jobs using his flail. He'd thresh a stack of oats for a shilling, and no matter what size the stack, he'd thresh it and quickly. He came along to Kirwan's place near Ballina and was employed there thrashing for a while. This day he thrashed away until he was called to dinner.

Now the stable man, who was a jockey for Kirwan's racehorses, was watching this man for some time seeing how easy it was for him to thrash. When the labourer was called in to his dinner, the boy carefully examined the flail and found that in the handle, with the other end being the beater, there was a screw top at the end of which held a dearga-a-daol (a black devil's coach-horse beetle). He took it out and put it in the saddle of one of the racehorses. Now, when the thresher came out after dinner and picked up his flail, he knew that he could thrash no more as he had before. He knew he had been tricked, and he didn't know who tricked him.

The stable boy who became a jockey went on to win every race after that on any horse he'd be on so long as he had that saddle under him. After a while, he was disqualified from riding in races as they suspected that there was something unusual or irregular about his riding, but they couldn't figure out what it was.

Once the Devil could take the jockey to any place he liked. Now, Kirwan once was hosting a fine party and the liquor started to run a bit short. He sent the jockey out on one of the racehorses to a public house for more liquor. He came back within a short time with French or German wine and brandy. There were some people there that evening that could read the labels of the foreign wines and wanted to know where the bottles were coming from. The jockey wouldn't give any account of where he got the bottles. Finally, the jockey's two favourite horses died on him and were buried in graves in Kirwan's, and when he was dying too, he asked to be buried between his two horses.[14]

⁂

The Baby That Came Through the Window

One evening a young man from Drumhuskert was out playing cards in Rossow near the Newport–Westport road, and he was coming home at a late hour. He was going down by Rosdoonaun, near the Rossow Bridge, and he seen a light in the window of a house in Rossow. Now, the light there didn't make any sense to him. He says to himself that there's something wrong in that house or there's someone sick for a light to be showing there at that hour of the night. He went on up to the window of the house and saw that there was a woman standing at the window with a little red cloak on her. As he approached the window, she moved to one side. Then she reappeared this time holding a baby in her hands, and she handed the child to him through the window. He took the child and walked off to his house in Drumhuskert.

His mother was in bed when he got to the house, and he says to her, 'Here's a child that someone will be looking for to-morrow.'

'Oh, you blackguard,' says she, 'is this what your night walking and rambling has brought you to at last.'

She thought it was how he had been misbehaving and that

some girl had brought him his own child to bring to his home. His mother wasn't a bit pleased about it and wouldn't listen to any of his explanations at all. She kept on grumbling and growling during the night thinking that she'd have to raise the child that belonged to her son.

Now the young man knew well that the child belonged to someone as he had gotten the child from someone else, and they'd be going looking for the child. That next evening, he walked off on his ramblings, and he walked again down to Rosdoonaun where he had got the child. As he talked to people there, he found out that a child had died there in this house the night before. So, he went up to the house.

'No child died,' says he. 'None at all. The missing child is safe above with me mother. Let ye go up and get him.'

They went back to check the cradle and found there was nothing in the cradle. It was empty. When they saw the cradle was empty, they were willing to believe him that the child was above in Drumhuskert. The mother and father marched off to Drumhuskert and brought their child back down with them. The poor young gambler went back to his card playing. The child grew up to be a man and managed to be just like all the country people in the country.[15]

✧

The Shadow That Changed the House

Once there was an ould man, Johnny, from Islandeady, and he had a family of four or five girls and one son. His only son died, and he was greatly upset over the loss. Not long after that one of his daughters, Maria, was going to Mass to the Islandeady chapel, and she fell on the road, and I remember this meself, and she died immediately or in a day.

Early one Sunday morning, Johnny had time enough to fix a gap in his fence that was bad before he'd go to Mass. He was cutting rods to fix up this gap, and he seen the shadow of a boy, like his son, on the other side of the fence. He was watching the shadow not expecting that it was to give him any information or anything, but the shadow spoke to him.

'Father,' the shadow says, 'you're in great trouble after Maria's death because your house is built in the wrong place, and you must make a new house in the track of the old drain where the water runs off the manure.'

Then, the shadow disappeared. Johnny went home with this secret, went to Mass and when he returned home, he went to work building a new house exactly where he was told. Now he wasn't very rich and in order not to lose any more members of his family, he went to the trouble of going to England to work on harvesting so that he could cover the expenses of building himself the new house.

I met Johnny when he was working in England, and Johnny explained that the problem with his old house was that it interfered with the fairies passing that way, as the house was in their way on their old route.

When Johnny was working at the new house, he'd dig four sods and call on the fairies to turn them down if they weren't in the right place. The fairies i'd do this in the night time. He wanted to make sure that there would be no humbugging in the future, for he knew that the fairies make humbug even in the middle of the day.[16]

The Child That Fell Out of the Air

Me mother's grandfather was Padraic Nolan, and he was married in Roscahill but lived in Collanmore Island, off Roscahill Point. One night, Padraic had to go in by the strand to his home, and he had to wait for the strand to dry up. He was going in by the rocks on Collan, and he heard a child crying over him in the air, and Padraic says, 'Cuir an páiste chugam a leanbh' (Give me the child, my dear). He opened his hands out, and a child was left in to his arms. Wearing long coats was common then, and he put the child in to the tail of his long coat and brought the child home with him in to Collan.

His old woman, Nancy Nolan, was in bed, and he says, 'There'll be someone looking for the child to-morrow, and we'll get the "proper owner for him"' (Seo, an páiste). She asks him to get a drop of milk and give it to the child. He told the woman how he got the child. There was only the two of them in the house then. She put the child beside her in the bed until the morning.

The next day Padraic came out of Collan to see where did the child belong. When he came to his daughter's house in Roscahill, she wanted to make a bit of food for him before she went to the wake house where this baby was dead since the night before.

He says, 'I'll have nothing now, but I'll go with you to the wake house.'

So, he went to the wake house with his daughter, and the people were gathering about for a little funeral to take the infant and bring it in a place they called Claggan.

'Bring me in a basket of turf,' Padraic says in the wake house, for they all knew him there. 'Bring me another,' he says, 'and bring another.' He made up a good fire quickly, and he took the shovel and split the fire in the middle.

'Why are you bothering about the fire now,' someone asks, 'with your building it up and then breaking it down again?'

Padraic says, 'I'll put what's in the cradle in there, and I'm going to set fire to whatever's in that cradle, and we'll have a better blaze when it lights up again.'

The mother was going wild with her crying when she heard this, and she tried to stop him. He went over to the cradle, and when he got there, there was nothing there but an ould brush or besom. They all felt bad now there was no child to be found there, neither dead nor alive and they were wondering what had happened at all. They threw out the brush in to the garden out of the way.

'So,' Padraic says, 'come on with me now to Collan and your child is within with Nancy.' There were four oars, and the boat was ready, and the four men, mother and father, and the old man went off for Collan. Nancy had the child within in Collan all safe and warm, and she sent their baby back home with them. The baby grew up to be a fine young man and went away to England to earn his living.[17]

༄

The Midwife and the Fairy Child

This old lady, Maire Gavan, was a midwife, better known as Máire na Roic. One night a man came on horseback to her house asking her to attend to a woman. She didn't know the man. She got ready and went along with the man sitting behind him but riding side saddle or cruppan.

When they were going along the man says to her, 'Don't take any food nor money of any description from the people in where I'm going to bring you.'

He brought her in to a fort or dún in a place called Rooghaun, near Croaghrin on the Tourmakeady road, the other side of Derrycraff. She attended to the woman. The child was born, and the minute the child was born, one of the crowd that was inside the house took the child and put it behind the fire. They all gathered around the midwife then giving her presents. They were all small little red-haired women that were in it, but the midwife took nothing of any description from them just as she was told. The man took her back again with him to her home on horseback as he brought her.

Near where Maire Gavan was living, there was another house that she had to pass, where an old blind woman lived, and there was a piece of straw in the window. Once as she was passing, the woman inside the house handed her out a child, and she saying, 'seo' (here). Maire took the child whispering, 'Is tu mo chuisle a mhic' (You are my darling son). She brought the child home and put the child between herself and the husband in the bed. The child never wakened all this time.

In the morning when Maire got up, she left the child sleeping in the bed. The next thing she heard was the neighbours shouting from their house, where the child was given out, that the child was dead. The mother, children and all in that house were crying mightily. Later, when the old midwife had her work at home done, she went in to the house where the child was dead.

When Maire went in to the house, she says to the mother, 'Your little child was overboard. What's on you?'

'Oh, me poor child,' mentioning the child's name, 'died last night.'

Maire went over and looked at the dead child, saying, 'Take that ould baby witch and throw it out.'

The bereaved mother went stark wild saying, 'How dare you say such a thing to my child.'

'I'll show you,' says Maire, 'whether it's your child or not.' She went over to where the child was left overboard and took whatever was in the cradle and put it behind the fire. It all went up in a blaze, and what hopped out of the fire but a little old man, and he ran out the door.

'Now,' says Maire, 'is that your child?' She then walked out and back to her own house and took up the child from where he had been sleeping and brought the child in to the mother.

'There's your child,' she says so the mother got her child back.[18]

⁂

The Hare of the Ridge Field

John Derrig lived in Knappagh Beg in Aghagower. He was a big powerful man and a thresher by profession, indeed a famous thresher and was also well known for cutting bog. An uncle of mine asked John to cut out or remove an old mound that was partly in the corner of a field that used to be in the way of the horses ploughing as they were turning the corner. They made a bargain for John to clear the corner for fifteen shillings.

'Faith,' he says in his own ould fashioned way, 'I'll soon earn that fifteen bob.'

In a few days John decided to start in at the work. He got his pick and spade and was getting on with it. He wasn't long working when he heard some queer noise. Now he wasn't a man to be easily cowed, and he didn't heed the noise at all for a while. He was still whacking away. After a while the noise got louder, and it distracted him from the work. He went away and stood looking back at the mound. He says to himself:

'I'm only a bloody coward to be haunted by that noise when I can see nothing. I'm not going to be put out of my work no matter what comes there.'

So back to work he went again. Now, he hadn't three blows of the pick struck again when he and his tools was taken and thrown out on the road. After that, for no amount of money, he wouldn't go back again at that work, and the mound is there still.[19]

The Hare That Became an Old Woman

Old Johnny Higgins was an old blacksmith, and he was bred and born in Aghagower, but he lived in Westport. He had two fine dogs, beautiful black dogs. One of them had a white spot and the other didn't. The one without the white spot was supposed to be the dog that's best fit to catch the hare. There wasn't a dog around in the country that hadn't tried to catch the hare. Now, this hare was sucking the neighbours' cows in Knappagh, and the cows used to become dry. Where now stands Jim Blaine's house there was another ould house, a kind of a racked old shanty, with a bit of straw shoved in the window when a storm would come, and an ould woman lived in it.

Johnny heard about the hare, and he went out to Knappagh with his two dogs. They gave chase to the hare, and the chase lasted for over an hour. They were both doing well keeping up with the hare. The black spot dog led the chase, but after a while the black dog got knocked out. The dog with the white breast continued on the chase, and he was getting close, almost on top of the hare. Now, when the hare came to the ould woman's house, just as the dog was about to nab him, the hare jumped in the window. The dog jumped in after the hare. Johnny was following them as fast as he could, and he came to the ould house and shoved open the door, searched the house high up and low down, but there was no hare to be seen – only the ould woman sitting in the corner there quietly.

Johnny says to the ould woman, 'The hare is not within the house if he's not under you.'

'Oh no,' says she.

Then, Johnny took and pulled the ould lady off her seat, and he found only a pool of blood under her. That finished the chase.[20]

The Man Found Spread-eagled on His Barn Roof

There was a mound out near Roughaun off the road near the village of Aghagower about three hundred yards from Aghagower Castle. There's a small little mound about six-foot high and on top of it there's a whitethorn bush about three-foot high. No one living remembers seeing it any smaller or any bigger. The whitethorn was never known to grow a leaf, but there was supposed to be a pot of gold under this little bush.

There's an ould man by the name of Dennis Moran who lived about five hundred yards from the mound with the whitethorn and one day he says to himself, 'I'll have a try for the pot of gold.' In broad daylight when he was digging away, and he was doing fine, until all of a sudden, he was lifted in to the air and brought and landed spread-eagled on the roof of his own barn.

At that time Dennis had a nice house, was a family man and had two fine boys and two good girls, and they were in a great health. Within six months of his digging, all his children were under the daisies in Aghagower.[21]

The Ould Man Dies at Sheean

There was an ould man named Haran who lived out at Sheean Hill, near the Castlebar–Westport road. On occasion when he was walking home late from a fair in Westport and had a drop taken and didn't feel like finishing the walk home, he used to knock at the door of this house, and they'd let him in, and he'd sleep there or at least get something to eat before he continued on his way.

Once on a cold and snowy night, he was walking home and felt that he didn't want to walk all the way home, and so he stopped at the house and knocked at the door, and no one answered. He started to beat on the door, but again, nobody answered. He was not feeling well, and so he sat down by the door and went to sleep.

Next morning, his dead body was found in the snow by the door.

After that, the family that owned the house would regularly hear a terrible noise pounding at the door and the voice of the ould man Haran calling out though he was long dead and buried. They didn't know what to do about the noise, and so they asked the local parish priest to read prayers for the dead and other things for Haran, but they didn't get rid of the noises. Finally, the family appealed to Archbishop MacHale to come to help them and give the house a special blessing. When he came, he had bits of written scripture, prayers and religious emblems, and he placed them in the corners of each room in the house. There was no disturbance from Haran after that. All was quiet. The ould man was finally at rest.[22]

∽

The Fairy Loom: Oliver Touser

There was a woman once who was well known in the area for her spinning of the yarn. One day a fairy came in to her, while she was spinning away, and he says to her, 'Will you have the yarn soon spun to take it over to the weaver?'

'I will,' says she. 'I'll have it spun and ready in a week's time.'

'Will you give it to me to weave?' says he. 'If you do, I'll make a nice piece of cloth for ye,' says he, 'and I'll charge you nothing for the weaving of it, but,' says he, 'you must tell me me name when I bring you back the woven frieze. If you don't, you won't get the frieze at all.'

In a week's time, your man comes back, and she had the yarn ready to go to the weaver in big bags. 'Remember you'll have to have me name when I come here with the frieze,' says he.

The woman let the yarn go and no bother. She thought that someone would be able to tell her the little man's name. She asked around, but nobody had seen him but herself, and nobody knew who he was. All she knew was that in a week's time, he was to bring her the frieze and she was to call him by his name. Now, the time was passing quickly, and she wasn't able to get any information as to who he was or what was his name. She was getting concerned in a bad way as the time was going on. Perhaps he was a tramp weaver who was collecting yarn for the people around. When the seventh day came, she still didn't know the weaver's name. Now that afternoon she happened to be up on the hill above her house, walking by a fairy fort, and she heard the buzzing of the loom inside.

'Begorrah,' she says, 'there's a weaver in there. If I could only get to see him, it might be the weaver that has me yarn.'

As she went further around the fort, she heard someone singing inside. The song she heard was, 'Is beag a shíleann bean an amhrais gur Oliver Touser mise' (The doubtful woman doesn't know that Oliver Touser is my name). She immediately thought that Oliver Touser is the little man's name. She was so happy.

'Begorrah,' she says, 'that's it. That's the weaver's name surely.'

She came down the hill full of joy and made sure that she didn't forget the songeen she'd heard. She was singing the song for fear that she'd forget it. She went on singing it through the house the whole of that night. The next day, when she got up, she was singing 'Oliver Touser' again. At ten o'clock who walks in with his frieze on his shoulder but the man.

'Well, says he, 'Cén t-ainm atá orm?' (What's my name?)

'Oliver Touser, deir an bhean' (Oliver Touser says the woman).

'Seo an rud anois' (Here it is now), he says giving her the piece of frieze. That frieze was by far better and exceeding the quality of any other frieze that was about in those days. He must have been a good friend of her that wanted to do such a job for her. Everything must be paid back one way or another.[23]

The Potatoes at Roscahill That Had Tracks of Teeth in Them

One time there was a family of four sons and their widowed mother living near Roscahill. The sons were all fishermen and were used to the hardy way of life on the sea. One evening the mother had put down the pot of potatoes for the supper to let them boil away. Suddenly, the four sons went out of the house just before sitting down to supper, and they were chatting away there outside by the wall, but they never came back in to the house to the supper. Shortly after that the mother went out wondering where they might be.

She'd seen the four of them leaning across the little wall outside the house. She called to them, but they didn't respond. They just disappeared. She was broken-hearted as she knew they had gone out on the sea, and they were drownded. From that time until the time she died, she put that same pot of potatoes on the fire every night boiling away, and she'd find part of the potatoes would be eaten and the track of teeth in the hard ones. The track of the blood would be left where the boys were munching on the hard ones.[24]

⁂

The Fairy Returns the Kindness

The man of the house was sick, and they were a long way from Westport. They had one pig for sale, and the woman had to go to Westport with the pig. Now, before she started off, she told the children how to take care of their sick father as he was in bed. Sometime during that prior evening two hens were killed, as they fell out of the loft or the cow lay on them someway. Before leaving that morning, she said to the eldest little girl to clean the two hens and have them ready when she'd come home and to make a drop of soup for the father.

She started off in the early morning in the moonlight with her pig and a rope on her until she came to this turn in the road, where there was a man standing. She didn't know the man, had never seen him before.

'Good morning to ye,' says he. 'You're on the road very early, too early for the market.'

'I am early indeed,' says she.

'Would you ever come in here to the house now with me, and I'll hold the pig,' says he.

'What would I go in there for?' says she.

'Musha, there's a young child inside,' says he, 'and the mother is gone, and would you suckle the child?'

She didn't like to go in, but she didn't like to refuse, and she knew she was early. In the end she went in and suckled the child. When she had done that, she came out, and he was there on the road still holding the pig. He told her that she should be going on the road now at her ease, to take her time, that she'd be early enough and that she'd have a good day at the market. She headed off, made it to the market and got more than she had expected for her pig.

'Well, now,' she says, 'I'm going to get home earlier than I expected for two reasons: first, for fear I'd meet that man again, and secondly, on account of me sick husband.'

She was going home alright, until she came to the same place where she had met the man in the morning, and there he was before her again. He asked her to do the same thing – to suckle the child in the house. Now, it was still full daylight and so she wasn't so much afraid of the man. She was thinking of excuses she could use to avoid the suckling.

'Where's the mother of that child? Isn't it fitter for her to be with her to suckle her and to look after her than for me?' says she.

'Well, herself and the little boy,' says he, 'is gone these two or three days looking for a cow to get a drop of milk for the child.'

He persevered on her. She was grumbling about her husband being sick and she hurrying home to him and that he was delaying her a second time.

'You'll be none the worse of it,' says he, 'and yer husband will be alright.'

She went in to the house a second time and did the suckling. Now when she was leaving, he wanted her to take a piece of meat with her for to cook for the husband. She refused and said that she had left orders for the two little girls to have the two fowl ready the time she got home.

'Well,' says he, 'you didn't kill them fowl.'

'Well, no, I didn't. The cow lay on them or something,' says she.

'Well, have nothing to do with them fowl,' says he. 'They'll be in the pot when you go home, and here's a little glass,' says he. 'Never, but never say anything about it or anything about how you came by it. When you get home,' says he, 'put this glass to your eye and look in to the pot, and you'll see what's in it, and your husband,' says he, 'will be alright. This will do him good,' he says. There's proof in it when he gave her the meat.

'Furthermore,' says he, 'from now on never eat anything that dies – and is not killed – as that belongs to us.'

She went away home, did as he told her, and found two sods of turf in the pot in place of the two hens.[25]

༄

The Man That Didn't Know Where He Was

Johnny Walsh at one time used to put up the lights for the boats on the perches in the ship channel. His first cousin, James Jordan, had come from Inishnakillew and was married up in Ballycarra, near Manula. One morning James was turning out his cows, and as he was looking about him over in the bogs in Ballycarra, he seen this man, and he went to him. When he got to him, he knew him for years. It was Johnny Walsh from the quay of Westport. James knew Johnny well for Johnny used to work in the lighters going up to the quay from Inishlyre.

'Johnny, Johnny, oh, what brought you here?' says James.

'Well. I don't know, James,' says he. 'Where am I?

'You're in the bogs of Ballycarra,' says James to him, 'and how did you get here?' says he excitedly.

'You know, I was in Mrs Gill's last night, and I was going home to Maria,' says Johnny, 'and then I found meself here. I don't know how I got here, but I didn't walk.'

'Well, come home with me 'til you have a bit of a breakfast if you want it?'

'No,' says Johnny. 'Am I near a railroad station, James?'

'Well,' says James, 'you're about two miles from Manula.'

'And what time is it?' says he.

'About ten o'clock,' James says, 'and there's a train going down at one o'clock. Have you money?'

'Oh,' says Johnny, 'I have plenty of money,' putting his hand in his pocket.

Johnny went home by train before the police and the people i'd be go out searching for him thinking he might be drownded. He lived to be an old man. James said it was the fairies that fetched him for he was a man that believed in fairies.[26]

The Bog-Deals That Were Tempered by the Fairies

Ould Walt Staunton lived in Cordarragh, in a part of Aghagower. He was a blacksmith. I remember him well and he was a friend of me family. His main way of making a living in those days was making bog-deal hatchets, slanes and horse shoes. The bog-deal hatchet is twelve to fourteen pounds weight. In the spring time, his bog-deals were in great demand. He used to work hard. A brother of mine used to work with him sometime, sledging away for he was a friend of the family, especially before market days as there was always a great demand for his bog-deals. Now, this Wednesday night before the market day, he got tired. He had a lot of bog-deals made, but he hadn't them tempered in time for the Thursday market in Westport. He was too tired to finish them off that evening. 'I'll go to bed,' says he, 'and get up early in the morning and have them tempered in time for the market.'

When Walt was going to bed, he heard a voice through the window asking him for a loan of the forge for the night. He says he thought they were tinkers that were passing there, and he thought what's the harm.

'It's there for you and make the best job you can out of it,' says he.

When he went out in the morning, he found all the bog-deals had been tempered and finished. Any man who bought one of those bog-deals that day found that it would withstand seven years hard digging while the ordinary bog-deal would only last one year.[27]

'Shooter' Moran and the Swan

There was a man in the neighbourhood of Ballinlough, near Westport, and he was a sort of builder and he was good at shooting, and he became known as Shooter Moran. If he heard that there was a hare or a bunch of duck anywhere within twenty miles of him, he'd go out for a shoot. Now, he was told that there was a swan on the lake by Ballinlough, and he told some of the boys that he'd shoot the swan, and he did.

Shooter Moran had a wife and a family of six children. Soon after the day he shot the swan, his wife died, and soon after that, two or three of the children died. Within twelve months of that day, there wasn't a member of his family nor a trace of his house anywhere around. He went over to England, and there was no trace of him after.[28]

Mickey Cooper and the One-Eyed Giant

Mickey Cooper was originally from Clare Island, but he came off it and was living in Louisburgh. It's said that he made up this tale.

One day Mickey had gone out to Clare from Louisburgh and was out footing turf on his bog lot there, when he heard a noise like a chain being dragged. Just then, he saw coming on up the hill towards him from the sea a tall man with one eye in the centre of his forehead as big as a watch. The man came up to Mickey and spoke to him. Mickey wasn't afraid of him at all.

'What's the name of this island?' asks the one-eyed giant.

'It's Clare,' says Mickey, thinking that the man was some kind of surveyor.

'Are you long on the island?'

'Yes,' says Mickey, 'I'm here ever since it was called Inisclara.'

The one-eyed giant looked at him and stretched out his hand. Mickey did the same, but the giant didn't take his hand.

'You're a bold one, but watch out man,' says the giant, 'and if ever I come on you by surprise, it'll be the worse for you.' Then he just vanished.[29]

Regatta, Roscahil, Westport, Co. Mayo, 1938.

CHAPTER 2

Lore of the Sea

⟨⟩

The Man Who Saw the Fairy General at Sea

IT WAS A VERY FINE night, and there were a fair number of fishing boats out on the bank, and there was nothing doing. They were hovering over a bank which was well known for good fishing, but this night there was nothing doing. No sight or sound of the fish, no bites or anything. Each of the boats had their nets out, and not one ever got so much as a bite. The word passed that the fish had gone further out to sea. The fishermen talked to one another and thought it was best if they pulled their nets up and went further out. They put their nets down again but with the same result – not a bite to be had. Once again, they were saying, 'Come on now, let's go further out to sea,' and they all followed. Again, they repeated this several times. There were still no fish, not even a bite.

They kept going out until they were outside Creggandilisk, which is sometimes called Pole Rock because there was a pole fixed permanently on the rock. The fishermen put down their nets again, and they felt for sure that they would get the fish this time. They were tired after all their moving, and they all went to sleep. There wasn't a murmur from any boat or from anyone. It was a calm night surely.

Now, Paddy Quinn from this island, who was me great grandfather's brother, was out in his boat, but he was not good at sleeping at night in a boat. Suddenly, he saw the sea around him all turning red and blood colour. It was repeated several times. The colours were striking and remained constant for some time. Paddy then saw this man in his uniform, like a general in the army, with his sword by his side, his feather out of his cap, and a red coat and short breeches. He was going from boat to boat and then walking away on the water. He came towards Paddy's boat but passed off it and didn't come in. Paddy wakened up his sleeping men.

'Now, boys,' Paddy says, 'let you pull up your nets. I'm afraid this will make a bad night.'

His men says, 'It'll be time enough when all the boats are going back.'

Paddy up and told them what he had seen. Now these three or four boats, from around Inishnakillew, were close together near Paddy, and they started to pull up their nets, and when one went pulling up, the rest went pulling up their nets.

One of the other boatmen further out noticed what Paddy was doing and cried out,

'Where are you going now, Paddy?'

'I'm going home,' says he, 'and anyone that wants to be safe tonight will follow me,' he says. 'This is going to be a bad night.'

The Inishcottle boat and the Collan boat followed Paddy in, and they went straight for home. He was only past the point by

Clynish when the storm came upon them. The other boats were all trying to pull up their nets in a hurry. The sea was already running so high that the waves were tumbling in to their boats, one wave on top of the other. Away out to sea, there were hundreds of fishermen drownded that night in the Murrisk waters. To make it plain that there must have been something mysterious in it, there were four men came in safe in to Bartrow, near Thornhill in Lecanvey, and went up under the bank and tied their boat. Then another boat with four men came in after them. The sea was running so mighty high that the four men that came in last, when they jumped out of their boat to bring her up on the bank to protect it from the rising tide, their boat rose up with the sea, and the four men was never seen again. Another four men swam to Clynish, and they were found standing dead against the door of a house the next morning.

Paddy believed that he was most fortunate and that the generalship of the fairies was indeed a good friend.[1]

The Fairies That Borrowed the Fishing Nets

Meself and me cousin, and Austin Quinn and his man, the four of us were in this boat, and we were out at the point of Inishlaughil. There was a light on Inishbollog, a big light, as big as a motor car light. Austin was the oldest of us, and he says, 'Boys, check to see whether any boats out from here are going in for shelter. There's a breeze blowing, it's growing, and it might not fare well.'

Austin knew what the light meant. We'd six nets out, and we pulled them all up. Then we pulled on towards the light as it was our way to come home in by the west side of Inishturk Beg, and up until we had come up to Rosstoohy, near the point of Rosmore.

'Now boys,' Austin says, 'you can throw out your nets there if ye like, and then we'll head for home.' By this time, there was a good breeze from the southwest. I remember it well. We let out six nets there, and we crossed Rosstoohy, right across a good herring place, and it was deep too, and we paid out two anchors with buoys. We bid our nets goodbye for the night, and we said we'd head for home. We came back to Inishnakillew, tied the boat up, and went home to bed.

In the morning the four of us went down again to the boat to go out and lift the nets to see what was in them. We went out to where we had put out our last anchors with the buoys. We looked about but could see no sign of any buoy. We looked everywhere around, but there was no buoy to be found. We knew we had six nets, but where could they have gone to? We pulled closer in to the land, and there we found the buoys. Well, we looked around and wondered how could the nets and buoys have found their way to the shore. Would they be tangled as we thought they might be. Well, it turned out that they weren't tangled at all. The six nets were laid out one beside the other in their full length. We pulled them in, and they didn't have a crab in them, nor a herring, nor a cobbler or gurnard, nor the little red fish. They were totally clean. This happened over seventeen years ago during the regular fishing season.

We knew then that the fairies had wanted to use our nets to go fishing with, and they were damned lucky to have the use of them free for the whole night. The fairies might have come from the ring fort by Rosstoohy, and they might have a spite against the people of Inishnakillew for they knew their actions too well.[2]

❧

The Mulloys That Gave Herrings to the Fairy Eel Fishers

Pat and Brian Mulloy, two brothers, belonged to Rosstoohy. They were out fishing herring at Ardagh, near Rosmore Point in Newport Bay, and they couldn't find any fish at all for all their effort. When they were on their way home, they came as far as the end of Inishcuill, just near Inishdaff, and they met a low boat with two men and a woman in her. They helloed them and asked them was there anything doing there. They did not reply, not a word at first, but then they ask the Mulloys, 'Where are ye coming from?'

'We're after coming back from Ardagh,' reply the Mulloys.

'Have ye any herring in yer boat at all?' they ask the Mulloys.

'We have only a few herring now,' the Mulloys reply.

'Would ye lend us even the few herrings ye have?' they ask.

The Mulloys pulled towards their boat, and when they saw who they had in their boat, they got afraid of them. They knew that they weren't of their class at all, but of the fairy tribe. Even so, they gave them a couple of dozen herring.

The people on the other boat thanked them and said, 'That was a generous gesture with the herring, and they would be enough as we're going off eel fishing.'

The Mulloys say they were going home.

The other boat reply, 'Go home for the evening, but if ye come out the next night to Rosstoohy, ye'd be sure to get a good load of herring, but that would be the last herring that ye'd catch for the rest of the year.'

That next night, the Mulloys went out fishing and got an enormous load alright, but that was indeed the last herring that anyone around got for the rest of the year.[3]

❦

The Fairy Mist

I was out with a group of islanders going to a mission or retreat in Kilmeena, and we all left our boats by the shore at Claggan. It was in September about twenty-five years ago. When we came back to Claggan after the mission, every man went to his boat and loaded up his people to make their journey home to their island. Now just as they headed off from Claggan, all of a sudden, this thick fog struck down on the top of us, and no one knew where to go. None of the island men could figure it out. The minute we went away from the shore, we didn't know where we were.

There was an old woman who lived here in Inishnakillew, Mary Máille, and she said that later that night, it was as bright and as clear as any day. She was looking out at the boats all across the bay as there were many boats all going home. The sea was covered with them. When the fog came down even on the islands, they lit fires down on the beach in a pot, and in every boat, there was a fire in their pot. It was so calm that night. The people believed that the fog came about because the fairies didn't wish to be going out of their own way when we were all going home, and so that's why they created this fog to blind us so that they could pass through on their own way home. The fog lifted after about only an hour, and there was the moon shining gloriously and not a cloud in the sky.[4]

⁓

The Fairies That Cheered up the Old Woman

About forty years ago two brothers, by the name of Gallagher, were set to sail a hooker to Westport from Achill. They'd go in to bring back cargo to Achill. There was no one living at home but themselves and their old mother. Now, the mother was expecting them back within three days, and they didn't come home. Their hooker boat was old, and the old woman was afraid they were lost.

By the fourth night she despaired of them ever coming home. Suddenly, there comes in a lot of youngsters, girls and boys, in to the house, and she knew them all, but she knew them to be dead. They were all enjoying themselves and having their music and fun, dancing and carolling as they used to be when they were young, and they took notice of her lamenting on her stool. 'Twas to cheer her up that they had come.

'So, cheer up Granny, and don't be so lonesome,' says one of them to her.

'Oh, how can 1 cheer myself up,' says she, 'when me two boys went to Westport Quay three days ago, and 1 was expecting them home, and they didn't come home to me, and I'm afraid they're lost.'

'Don't be afraid, Nanny, for yer boys,' says one lad. 'There was a big battle fought for them,' says he, 'and our party was stronger than the other, and we defeated them. All they could do,' says he, 'was to put the boat on a rock, but there's nothing wrong with the boat. The spring tide is on the rise now,' says he, 'and the boat will float off the rock, and they'll be here in two days more,' says he. 'Don't be uneasy about them,' he says, 'for we had charge of them, and we'll be able to master the other party at any time. That was the other party of fairies that wanted to drown them. We'll come back again to-morrow night, and we'll comfort you 'til they come home.'

They did come the next night, and she knew every one of them for they were all Achill boys and girls.[5]

⌒⌘⌒

The Phantom Ship's Boat off Inishshark

In 1860, about eighty years ago, a fleet of about twenty-five fishing boats went out herring fishing on a fine day in August from Aughris, near Cleggan, to Inishbofin and Inishshark, and they foregathered in the fishing grounds inside the safety of Shark. In some of the boats, there was a crew of five, but others had only four. Each boat had long trains of nets, and they set them in the evening.

When the fishermen had their work done early in the evening, it began to grow dark, and suddenly they saw a big light coming towards them from the mainland, and it came on pretty fast.

Naturally, they wondered what it might be, but they weren't left long in doubt. It resolved itself into a ship's long boat, carrying twelve oars, with six men pulling on each side. Some of the fishermen hailed the boat as it passed through their midst, but there was no response from the boat at all. It came in right through the little space there was between the boats. All of them saw it, and it passed right out to sea. They were sure that there was no ship of any kind to be seen.

Immediately after its passing, a little breeze came along, followed by a strong blow, and then followed by a fierce gust of wind. The sea became choppy and wild, and waves began to dash in to the boats. In a few minutes the position looked very ominous, and it appeared that they were in for a bad night. Some of them rushed to cut the ropes of the nets to clear them away as they saw danger coming in on top of them. Suddenly, a big wave rolled in on their boats, filled them up, and they sank. One of the men managed to grab an oar, and he was taken away with it but managed to hold on. The wind blew him towards Bofin, one and a half miles away, and after some time, he lost consciousness.

On account of the storm, the people of Bofin gathered around as they were anxious about their own boats. They went down to the strand, and before them, they saw this man clinging to an oar as he had been carried in by the tide. They took him in, carried him to the nearest house and applied first aid to him. Eventually he was brought to and survived. He was the only man of all of them that went fishing out to sea that was saved that night. His two brothers were drownded as were all the neighbours.[6]

The Flax Threshers Under the Sea

Just before sunset one evening, there was an ould man out with his two partners, and they were out dredging oysters down at Inishbollog. The two men were pulling on their oars, and the third man was behind in the stern holding onto the dredging rope with the dredge down on the floor of the sea. Suddenly, the dredge got caught on the bottom.

The dredger says to his comrades, 'We have no dredge,' meaning it was stuck below. 'I'll have to go down on the rope and liberate it. It must be that it's stuck under a rock.'

He caught hold of the dredging rope, and slipped down on it until he got down to the bottom to find the dredge was caught under the threshold of a door below, and the door was open. The man looked in to the house and saw that there were two men threshing the clefts of wheat with their wooden flails tied together inside on the floor.

'God bless yer work,' says he.

'And you too,' says they. 'Arrah, then you're welcome.'

'I wouldn't have come down here at all,' says he, 'but me dredge was caught in the threshold of the door.'

He didn't really know where he was. He was so mesmerised. He went up to the fire, and he turned round with his back to the fire, and he seen this toothless ould man within in the bed in the cailleach built out from the wall, and he says, 'What's wrong with you that you aren't flaying the straw, and it getting night.'

'I would indeed be flaying it,' says he, 'only for you.'

'What have I done to ye?' says he.

'So, you struck me yesterday with an oyster shell,' says he. He had a big gash in the forehead right over the eye.

'How could I do that to ye?' says he.

'Do you remember the seal that was swimming round you yesterday evening, and you threw an oyster shell at him, and you struck it here?' he says pointing to his head. 'And that was me. Be going away now with ye,' says he. 'It'll be night when ye'll be at home, and don't be so fond of pelting at seals anymore.'

The dredger liberated his dredge, and up he went on his rope. When he got up in to the boat, his partners thought it was drowned he was, when he wasn't coming up for so long. One of them says to him, 'What were ye doing down there?'

'Well, I was in this house below,' says he, 'and there's two men threshing in it,' and he told them the whole thing he had seen. They weren't believing him. Indeed, it was hard to believe such a story. So, the dredger jumped out of the boat again and went down on the rope. He remembered the lads down below had been threshing, and so he found a sheaf of oats and brought it back up with him. The sheaf of oats proved his point to the men in the boat, and he threw the sheaf overboard. The next day when he was going fishing, he noticed that the hens in Inishcottle were eating the oats which he had thrown out.[7]

✳

The Seal That Spoke Irish

Me grandfather, Michael Quinn, often told me this tale. He had a large sized boat, a hooker, and was seven or eight tons, and she used to bring turf from Achill. One day when they were coming in from Achill, near the white strands of Mallaranny, they looked out and seen a fair going on under the sea below them. People were buying and selling cattle, making bargains, and clapping hands as we do.

They sailed on a bit further, and they picked up a young seal that was tangled in their nets. The seal's mother followed the boat all along 'til they landed the young seal in on the dock. They took her out and brought her to the house, which was near the shore, and they put her in the cupboard. Now, there was a half stone of oatmeal already placed in the cupboard where the young seal was put, and the seal started eating it, and didn't she start to choke on the dry oatmeal. She called out to her mother in Irish crying, 'Mata, Mata! Tá me anseo a mháthair' (Mother, I'm here, mother). Her mother responded back to her from below on the shore. So they took down the seal to the shore when they heard her speaking Irish. The mother threw her up in the air seven or eight feet high catching her again until they left sight.[8]

The Man Who Caught the Mermaid

There was a man from Clare Island who was off fishing, standing on a rock with his rod and line. He noticed that this young seal woman came in under the rock near him, and she began to bathe – to wash herself. He moved across the rocks to be near her and went to talk to her. She answered him back as she had the talk. They talked for a good while. She left her comb near him on the rock, and he went and took it. He took the comb with him and headed for home, and she followed him. He brought her to his house. They lived together there, and I suppose they got married. She looked to be a fine young woman, and they had three or four children in their family.

He had her comb hid in the thatch of the house, where she wouldn't find it, and she wouldn't leave without it. One time when the man was off fishing, some accident happened in the house, and the house took fire. When the fire spread, it got up in to the thatch. She got the smell of the burning of the comb, and she ran up a ladder to where it was, took it out and went off to the sea again with it. For years after, those children used to go down to the strand. She'd come in on the strand to meet them and wash and comb their hair until the tide would come in covering her, and then they'd go home.[9]

The Clare Island Drownding – 1

One of the worst drownding disasters around Louisburgh happened when six men were drowned in December of 1883. There were four O'Malleys from Clare Island, a Moran boy, and a McHale boy from Emlagh. They were after bringing cattle in the boat off the island, and they didn't have any ballast to put in on the bottom of the boat for the return trip. Instead of lying down on the bottom, the men sat on the seats, and they were all drownded when the boat turned over.

An O'Toole man from Emlagh was going back on the boat with them, but when he got up in the morning, he couldn't find his shoe. He searched all around for the shoe and finally found it, but just as he got down to the quay, he saw the boat sailing off to Clare.

The Congested District Board's boat, *The Wasp*, from Westport passed to the west of the boat that morning on its way to Inishturk, and they saw the boat bottom aloft, but they never came to help them.

It was a fine day. The wind was straight after them, and the steerer, the Moran boy, could let the wind out of the sail. His father was a pilot, and he used to take men out in the boat instead of ballast, but he made them lie on the bottom of the boat. Young Moran didn't understand this, and he let the men sit up on the seats. The boat was only a mile from shore when it overturned.

A brother of the Moran boy drownded at the Clare lighthouse in that July, when he slipped out of the boat at Carraig Gaon. He struck his head on a rock, and he was drownded. They sold that boat to an Achill man. Pat Lavelle of Achill had built the boat there, and he was awful anxious to get the boat back, and he wouldn't let up with Moran 'til he bought the boat back, but he never put foot in the boat after that.[10]

❧

The Clare Island Drownding – 2

In the year 1883 Anthony O'Malley and his brother, Michael, of Clare Island and four other men went out to the mainland on some cattle business. The O'Malley men went to stay in their father-in-law's house, Austin McHale, to spend the night and their brother-in-law, McHale, agreed to go in with them. In the morning they got up early and went down to the harbour at Roonah, and on the way they called to an O'Toole man from Emlagh, who had slept in another house, to come along. He was in bed but got up quickly and put on his clothes, but when he was looking for his stockings, and couldn't find one of them. After some time, he found the other stocking under his bed, and he rushed out after his friends to the harbour, but when he reached it, they were sailing away into Clare.

That 28th of December was a fine day as it started. Their boat was a yawl and light in ballast. It capsized and the men were never seen alive again. She had brought in a heavy load of cattle, which acted as ballast, and she had no ballast as she was going back. The men sat down to balance the boat, but they were not like ballast. She was upset by a squall. The Coast Guard gunboat passed along in or about that time on its way to Inishturk, but there's no evidence to show that she saw the wreckage.

Later that day there was bad weather, and the storm continued for three weeks without ceasing. It wasn't possible to go out to search for survivors. One great tide came in the like of which wasn't witnessed for a long time. It came in to parts of the land by the house that were never touched by water before.

The bodies of the two O'Malleys and McHale came ashore around at Carrowmore. McHale's remains were taken home, and the O'Malleys, Anthony and Michael, were brought to the Louisburgh church. The two of them were brought in together in a box as a coffin. They had a brother living in Louisburgh who identified the remains. They held a wake in his house that night.

The local parish priest at the time, Father William Joyce, ordered the lights of the church to be put out when the church was closed, and as he was going to bed, he noticed that the windows of the church were brightly lighted up. He went down to the clerk's house and inquired of his wife where he was.

'He's at the wake,' she says.

The priest sent for the clerk, and he asked him why didn't he put out the lights in the church.

'I put them out as you told me, Father,' he says.

The priest and the clerk went up to the church, and when they unlocked the door, they found only the sanctuary lamp burning, nothing more. They went out then and locked the door again, and when they got outside, the church seemed to be just as bright as ever. The priest said it was better to leave it alone.[11]

The Drowned Man That Wanted a Burial

There was a herring fishery in Pol a Walky, off the south side of Cloghcormick, between that and Rabbit Island. There was usually a good take of herrings going there. One day when the fishermen pulled in their nets, they pulled in a drownded man. They went out a piece away from the fishery and dropped him out again, and they let out their nets again far away from where they had dropped the body. The next time they pulled in their nets, didn't they pull in him in again. This time they went further away now and again dropped him out. They came a half mile away and set out their nets again.

When they pulled their nets again for the fourth time, they pulled him in again. Now, these were wise men and proper fishermen, and they thought together, and said, 'This man wants burying.'

Then they went in through the waters between Inishbee and Cloghcormick, and they brought him to a point of Inishbee called Gob Dubh. They landed there, went up the hill, and looked for a spade to dig a grave and got it from the Gavins, who were living there then. They dug a grave for him, put him down in it, covered him up properly and they went again to fish, and he never troubled them anymore. All he wanted was a proper burial, that was his wish.

They got four to five hundred herrings in a shot of an hour; if they left the nets out any longer, the fish would be dying on them because they would be getting tangled up in the meshes of the nets.[12]

∾

The Drowning of Tom Purcell of Bofin

There once was a fisherman by the name of Thomas Purcell, and he belonged to Bofin. He married a lady, and they lived in Collanmore off Rossmindle and had a boy child. He was fishing all the time and was an able fisherman too. One time he was out fishing by himself and drownded.

Many years later one evening, and it was a kind of a dull evening, the widow Purcell was outside of her house and the shadow of a man appeared, but she went on with her business and didn't take any more notice. The next time the shadow appeared to her, he was a full man.

'Don't be afraid of me. I'll do you no harm,' says Thomas.

'Of course,' says she to him. So, she cheered up. 'Oh. Thomas, oh. How long have you been here?'

'I'm here all the time now since I was drownded, and I had great shelter while that ould barn was still up there,' says he, 'but then it got pulled down.'

'What do you want me to do for you, Tom, oh?' says she.

'Me son now is fourteen years,' says he, 'and he must earn the price of three Masses for me and pay for them for me. My brothers are to be at Westport Quay on Tuesday next, and tell them about it, and they'll take me son with them to Bofin, and they'll go fishing the next day. When they go home to Bofin on Thursday, they'll give him a line, and every fish he catches, he should keep them and sell them for himself. When he has the price of the three Masses, sold in fish, let him give the price of the Masses out of his earnings to the Bofin priest, and after the Masses are said, I'll be no bother to anyone in this world. I'll be soon in Heaven then.'

Wasn't that joyful news! Herself and her son went to Westport Quay on the Tuesday and met Tom's brothers and told them the whole story as it was. They had to spend their day in the market in Westport, but the next day they took the boy with them to Bofin. When they went fishing, they weren't an hour fishing, but the boy caught more than enough fish for the money that was called for to say the three Masses. He paid the Bofin priest enough for the three Masses, and the brave poor man, Tom Purcell, that was dead for those many years was released from Collanmore for evermore.[13]

The Foretelling of the Ship That Sank

John Máille of Islandmore went away from the island, and he landed a job as the second mate on a ship and was also the ship's carpenter. He saved up his wages and had some money when he'd come home to his brother in Westport. Now that money wouldn't last long as he spent it fast enough.

In late 1939 he wrote home about an incident in a saloon in Liverpool, where he was out drinking with the crew of the ship he was about to go out on that night. A man came in to the saloon, and no one knew him, and he asked for a drink from the sailors, but he was refused. They only laughed at him for they had their bellies full of beer, and so he went out. John Máille decided to go out the door after him.

'I'll buy you a pint,' says he, 'or the price of it.'

'You're going to sea with them fellows?' the man says to John.

'I am,' says John. 'We're going on the ship that's going out of here to-night.'

'Don't go on that ship for she'll get lost,' the man says.

John went back in to the saloon and told the crew what had happened and that he wouldn't be going out with them that evening, but they carried on anyway. The ship went out that night and was lost out at sea soon after she left Liverpool. All her crew were drownded. It wasn't by mines she was sunk! That pint of beer saved good-hearted John Máille for he didn't value money more than his life. This world is only a shadow and if one has it good, then one shouldn't add the length of a finger to one's days.[14]

The Warning Voice from the Dead

Joe Kelly of Islandmore was on a schooner out at sea, and one night a strong wind came up suddenly, and it was hard to keep the boat on a steady bearing because of the rough seas. The sails began to flap against the riggings.

The captain says to Joe, 'Joe, you go forward and pull in the forward jib sail.'

Joe went out on the deck and up on the foot rope out by the bowsprit to tackle the sail. Just then he heard a voice saying to him, 'Joe, go in out of that at once.'

Though he was only a year old when his mother died, he knew it was his mother's voice telling him not to go out further for the sails but to go back in. He returned in from the bowsprit, and he wouldn't go out again. The captain then sent out another man and wasn't he swept away in to the sea.[15]

The Dead Father That Saved the Boat

There was a blacksmith that lived in the village of Askillaun, near Louisburgh. His name was Matthew Gordon, and he liked to fish. His father was drownded not too far out in Clew Bay when Matthew was only a few years of age.

When Matthew was a grown-up man, he was one afternoon out fishing in the bay with a few others in a boat. Suddenly, as the evening was coming on, a storm started to brew, and it got dark. By the time they had their nets in and had started for home, the wind and rain had overtaken them. The storm was so intense that after a while they lost their way. They didn't know where they were going. Matthew was in poor shape, as he remembered his father had drownded in the bay many years before. They wandered around in the storm for a good while and still did not know where they were going. At last, they heard the roar of breakers quite close to them, and suddenly he saw a light shining in a kind of a sandy cove. It was held by someone, but he could see only a hand. Then he saw the features of the man holding the light, and they were those of his dead father. He turned their boat in at once to the little cove, and they were saved. There is only one cove between Cragganbaun Strand and Carrowmore, and there's also a little sandy cove at Pulgloss.[16]

The Whale That Swallowed the Man in the Boat

There was a fellow, Seán Rua Kane of Roeillaun Island, near Mallaranny, who was out fishing one day in a small boat from Inishnakillew. Seán was out with a standing line, fishing cod at the rocks off Roeillaun. Suddenly, this monster whale rose up out of the sea and swallowed Seán and his boat, with him inside in it.

Seán had plenty of room in the belly of the whale, but as he was settling down all of a sudden, he started to get hungry. He looked around and wondered what he could do. Now, he had a little fire in the bucket in the boat and so he took out his knife and cut a piece of the whale's meat which he thought would be fit to eat. He set to and cooked something of a meal for himself and liked it well enough. Now, when the whale started to smell his own fish flesh being burned, he went and took off out to sea to try to dislodge the fisherman.

About this time the whale fishers were active fishing whales round at Inishkea, off Belmullet. It was Seán's lucky day for didn't they harpoon this whale, and the whalers tied him up well to tow him in to the port. When they brought the whale on shore and opened him up, didn't they find Seán sitting inside there within his little boat and his little fireen was still burning.[17]

The Bull That Helped to Get a Wife

Once there was a young fellow, Seán, in Inishnakillew, and he was courting a girl, Maria, out on the mainland. He was in love with her, and she was in love with him, but her parents weren't satisfied with him. Didn't her parents plan to get her married to a man in the village to which she belonged. Now Seán was visiting in his neighbour's house on the island, and they'd chat for many an hour. This evening when he came visiting to the house, the woman of the house says to him, 'Musha, Seán,' says she, 'as long as you're a-courting, your woman is being married today to another on you.'

'To whom is she getting married?' asks Seán.

'To such a one from her own village on the mainland,' says she.

'Bad enough,' says he. He put a coal to light his pipe, and he walked out.

There was a man in the island that kept a bull, and this bull would often take a swim out to the mainland. Seán got his stick and went to where the bull was, drove him in to the tide, caught him by the tail, and kept the bull headed for the mainland where Seán was wanting to go. When he got out there, he let the bull go wherever he liked, and he went off to the house where he used to visit Maria, the woman with whom he was in love.

The woman of the house says to him, 'As long as you're a-courting, your woman is married today on you.'

'Where's Maria?' says he as she was the daughter of the house.

'Musha, she was here a while ago,' says she.

'Tell her,' says Seán, 'that I want her, but be sure and tell no one now but herself.'

Maria came to meet him, and she didn't tell anyone in the wedding house.

'Will you go for me, ould sweetheart?' he asks her. 'I'm here and don't want anyone but yourself.'

Now, it was a custom in those days to have a wedding breakfast before the marriage. Seán and Maria spent the night before the breakfast together in conversation the same as they always did, and the poor fellow was honest about it surely.

Later, Maria's family missed her. 'Where's she gone to out of the house?' somebody says. 'Where's Maria?' and like that the word went around, and she wasn't to be seen. Maria didn't come back until it was quite late that night. A report also went around that Seáneen was in the village.

Now, the young man who was expecting to get married heard

the rumour and became very disagreeable looking and cranky, and the wedding was near to being upset. The wedding was to go on that next day, but that was no comfort to him. The mainland fellow kicked up such a fuss, and finally said he wouldn't have her at all. A fellow tried to console the man and managed to keep him quiet for a while. Then the young man went and explained the case to the priest.

'What am I supposed to do?' says the priest. 'It's between ye.'

By this time many there were middling warm with drink, and one of the old men made this remark. 'I don't see what ye can do about it, as the little marriage might well be already done by now.'

Those words put an end to the wedding. The young man called it all off. Seáneen got his woman, and they gave him a big fortune, and he brought her back to Inishnakillew.[18]

Races on the strand, Carrowmore, Louisburgh, Co. Mayo, 1938.

CHAPTER 3

Heroic Tales and Anecdotes

⤔

Dearg Mór

DEARG MÓR CAME TO INVADE Ireland from the Eastern World or Domhain Thoir. Because of his tooth of wisdom Fionn mac Cumhaill knew that Dearg Mór was coming and had undertaken to prepare and train his two best champions for this fight – his own son, Rinnin Roe mac Finn and Ceol Croige mac Craven. While they were preparing for battle, they were training even more than they had before. They awaited the arrival of Dearg on the seacoast somewhere near Dublin. While at exercise one day, Finn's son said in a loud voice so people around could hear him, 'There's no man alive that I amn't able to master in single combat.'

Ceol Croige replied, 'I hope it's true for you, Rinnin. Those words are sweet from your lips, but only if your rival was getting tired during the struggle would I agree with you.'

After some time Dearg arrived in Ireland alone in his boat. He jumped to the shore, caught his boat under his arms and drew it up a considerable distance on the beach. The two champions approached him, one on either side. Dearg took them both down, tied their hands and bound them together. Then he secured his boat and took them, one under each arm, to the court of Cormac mac Airt.

When the assembled court saw Dearg coming with their two champions already crushed, they got very much afraid and cried out to Cormac with fear that they'd all be killed. Cormac pacified them and told them to have patience until he'd see what could be done.

Dearg marched in to the court and demanded the surrender of Ireland to himself.

Cormac announced: 'Our sovereignty has often been challenged by those coming across the salt waters but has never yet been given to an invading army with hundreds of soldiers much less given to one man.'

Dearg answered, 'If all your champions were mine, be they gentle or simple, high or low degree, not one man of them would I bring with me to fight across the sea. But I tell you this, I mean to have the sovereignty of Ireland for myself alone, and I'll build a wall around this island with all the dead bodies of your champions by the simple force and power of my blows.'

Then, Cormac picked out fifty champions and sent them off to fight, and they lost. Then another fifty, one set of fifty after another, until five hundred champions were killed.

Cormac called on the Fianna to help.

When Dearg saw the Fianna coming in their awesome strength, he said to Cormac: 'If it is to fight me that this rabble is coming from the mountains of Leinster, I pity their chances of ever returning there.'

Dearg fought the Fianna, and soon they were nearly annihilated. Then Fionn sent for Goll mac Morna. Goll at this time had fallen out with the Fianna and was somewhere in Connaught well away from them. At first Goll refused to consider taking part in the defence of Ireland because he said he had been badly treated by the Fianna previously.

'If we had not been burnt with fire and badly treated,' said Goll, 'I would give you my help, but now I won't.'

The messenger reported back to Cormac and Fionn and then returned again with their promises of riches and lands for Goll and pleaded with him not to allow one man to conquer Ireland for himself. Goll changed his mind and dressed himself from head to foot for the first time in his life in his armoured plates and coats of mail and returned to Cormac's court to help fight Dearg in single combat.

The fight started and showers of sparks and smoke rose up from their armour as the two men fought and clashed. They fought to a draw nine times, and on the tenth fight, everyone that was watching the whole time was very much interested and greatly concerned about the outcome. Finally, Dearg was felled by Goll's hand, and as he was dying, Goll said, 'It's a pity I hadn't my brother here, the blows of one sledge are slow' (Is mall buille an oird/cheapoird).

When it was all over and Ireland was saved from Dearg by Goll, Cormac and Fionn broke their promises to Goll, and instead of rewarding him, they chained him to a rock under a cliff, where he drowned. They felt then as they had before that Goll could not be trusted even though he had saved Ireland.[1]

Gobán's Son Shortens the Road

Gobán was a mason and was well known for his skills in building grand houses and castles. He lived with his wife and son, and his son would help him in the building. Once he was asked to build a great castle for a lord, and he agreed and took his son with him.

On the first day, the father and son started off on their way to build the castle, and they went on the road. They went on only so far, and the father turned home again and the son with him.

The next day they went on their way again walking, and the father says to the son:

'Why don't you shorten the road for us?'

'How can I shorten it?' says the son.

'Well, if you can't,' says the father, 'we'll have to go home for the journey is too long.'

When they went home, 'Are ye coming home again?' says the old mother to the son.

'We have,' says the son. 'Father wanted me to shorten the road for him,' says he, 'but how could I shorten the way?'

'Couldn't you tell him little stories, little Gubo,' says she, 'and it would be shortening the road?'

They started off on the third day, and before they came to where they had stopped the day before, the youngster went on and started telling a story to his father, and the father listened to him with great attention, and when he had that one told, he went on with another. Then the old man went and told a story. So, they didn't turn home any more on their journey 'til they reached their journey's end at the lord's place.

They went on then and started building the castle. They worked away at it for seven years and seven days. Now, when he had the castle almost finished, the lord says to Gobán one day, 'There's no castle now in Ireland like that,' and then he says to Gobán, 'Now, Gobán, have ye the castle finished?'

'Oh, no,' says Gobán, 'not yet. There's a tool at home in me box, and it won't be finished 'til I get that tool. I can't finish it 'til I get me tool. I'll send me son for the tool,' says he.

'Oh, no,' says the lord, 'my son will go for it. What's the name of it?'

'Curran in an cur agus cammer in an can' (twist against a twist and take again a turn).[2]

So, off goes the lord's young son on his charger until he got to the ould woman's house. The ould woman met him. She knew there was something on, and he says, 'I come from Gobán. I'm lord so and so's son. There's a tool in his box,' says he, 'and I came for it.'

'What's the name of it?' says she.

He says, 'Curran in an cur agus cammer in an can.'

There was a high box in the workshop where Gobán kept his materials. She put a stool outside the box and says, 'Stoop in there now and pick it up. I can't reach it.'

When she got him standing on the stool and leaning over in the box, she put her hands under his legs and hopped him in to the box. 'Stay there,' she says, 'until Gobán and me boy comes home to me.'

She ordered the lord's son to write his father that she would make him a present of his son when Gobán and her son would come home. When the lord got the writing, he put horses on his carriage and delivered Gobán and his son back home, and he took away his own son with him. When the lord was leaving, Gobán says to him, 'Now, you can put as many improvements as you like on your castle for I can go no further.'[3]

Young Gobán Finds a Girl for Himself

Ould Gobán got married to his wife, and soon they were expecting a child. Now, the first birth was a female child. At about the same time there was another woman, living just near to them, and her first child was a man child. Didn't the two midwives change the children, and they took Gobán's female child and left Gobán's wife with the man child. It all fared well, and didn't they grow up, a fine girl by the other woman and the man child made a fine stócach 'til he got to be a full boy, and he grew up to be marriageable.

One day didn't Gobán send his son out with a sheep's skin full with its wool to sell and get the price of it, but he failed.

The second day, Gobán sent him out again with the same full skin, and he got a woman to bid him for the wool and to give him back the skin and the price of it.

On the third day, Gobán sent him off again with another pelt with him and didn't he meet a young lady in a stretch of the road washing clothes.

'Well, young man,' says she, 'I seen you passing here so many days ago, and what's yer business,' says she, 'that you're on the road?'

'I have a full sheep skin,' says he. 'I want the skin back and the price of the wool, and I can get no one to give it to me.'

'Show me the sheep's skin,' says she.

So, he shows it to her. When she examined the skin, she took it with her in to the house, got a shears, and didn't she clip off the wool of the hide and rolled up the skin when she had the wool clipped off it, walked out to the young man with it.

'Here now,' says she, 'the skin and the price of it to you.'

When the son landed home, Gobán says to him, 'How did you do today?'

'Faith, I done alright,' says he. 'I got back the skin and the price of the wool today.'

'That's alright,' says Gobán. 'Do you know who gave it to you?'

'I do,' says the son. 'It was a young lady that gave it to me.'

'Keep your eye on that one,' says Gobán to the son.

Sometime after, didn't Gobán send his son out for to pick up a wife for himself, and says he, 'Don't forget the one that gave you the skin and the price of it. Keep your eye on her.'

Didn't the two of them turn over and get married, himself and the girl.[4]

⚬

Young Gobán's Wife Saves Her Father, Gobán Saor

Old Gobán knew well that young Gobán's girl must be a cute hoor, and that she was his real daughter.

The young Gobán and his wife lived away from his father for a good bit. Old Gobán heard talk of this big palace to be built in England, and he says to the son, 'What do you think? Will we beat the road for it?'

The castle was getting ready for being built and advertisements were out for special masons, real mechanics, and others.

'Alright,' says the son.

So, they packed up one morning and set out on the road but young Gobán's wife says to him, when he was leaving the house, 'Have the women on your side wherever you'll go.'

'Let you shorten the road,' says the father to young Gobán.

'How in the world,' says he, 'can I shorten the road?'

'Well then,' says he to the son, 'let us turn home.'

So, when they landed in, Gobán's wife asked the son, 'What happened?'

'Me father told me to shorten the road,' says he.

They set out the next day on their journey again.

'Shorten the road,' says Gobán to the son.

'How can I?' says he.

They turned home once again the second day, and the wife asked him, 'What's up again?'

'He told me to shorten the road again,' says he.

'Ah you fool,' says she, 'why didn't you begin telling stories and talking about buildings?'

They started off again on the third day. 'Shorten the road,' the father says to the son.

'Father, how long do you think it'll take us to get there?' asks the son.

'Sorra one of us can tell you rightly,' the father says.

'It must be a great building, father,' says the son, 'that we're making for. I believe,' says he, 'that it's going to be the finest in the world according to the pedigree of it. Do you think will they pay big wages for it?' says he.

'Well, I don't know,' says the father, 'until we reach there.'

'Well, I wish we were there now,' says the son. 'We're getting very tired.'

So, they landed up there at the site at last.

'Will we get in, father?' says the son.

'Faith, we might,' says the father, 'if we have good luck.'

Right away, they up and asks for a job. This big lord comes out and asks them, 'What can ye do?'

'We can do what any man can do,' says Gobán.

'Could you,' says one of the head masons that was in it, 'make a cat with two tails?'

'I might do that same,' says the ould Gobán.

So, they were all called as the dinner hour had come on, and they were asked to have their dinner. Gobán says, 'There's time enough yet for myself and my son here.'

It was an hour before the dinner. Anyway as soon as he could Gobán got there in to the dinner and then didn't he set to work to make the cat with two tails. When they come out from dinner, wasn't it placed on the corner of the building, the cat with two tails. Didn't he work it well and to have it finished in that time. The beat of Gobán never balked, they say, for any plan he laid out, he could go through it. When the high lord hears about the cat with two tails being made, he sacks every blooming maneen that was going to be set to work there and keeps Gobán and the son there 'til they finished the last particle of it.

The lord says, 'It will be six months before the castle will be completed, and then I'm going to behead them,' says he, 'before there's another like it built.' He says that to the company within at their supper one night. Gobán was within in another room sleeping. Wasn't one of the servants around and didn't she hear the conversation going on. Didn't she up and tell Gobán's son the plan that was going on, and he was maybe kind to her. Gobán got that advice from his son.

When Gobán had the castle almost finished, the lord comes out to him, and he looks around at it and views the whole of it.

'Is the palace finished?' says the lord to Gobán.

'It is,' says he. 'It's finished, but for one tool I have to have to finish it with – "Curran in an cur agus cammer in an can".' (Twist against a twist and take again a turn.)

'And how will you get that tool?' asks the lord.

'Your son and mine,' says he, 'can get it and go straight off to Ireland for it.'

'Oh, Lord,' says the lord, 'I thought it was finished.'

The lord straight off got his own son and Gobán's son to make the trip. As soon as they land at the house, Gobán's wife seen the son, and she hadn't seen him for six months. Of course, she would have been happy to see her husband.

'We have a message,' says the son to the mother, 'for a tool,' says he, 'that's here in the house.'

'What tool is it?' says she.

'Curran in an cur agus cammer in an can,' (twist against a twist and take again a turn) says the son. 'We were going to be beheaded as soon as the castle was finished, meself and me father,' says he.

'Oh, Lord,' says she to him, 'why were you going to beheaded?'

'For fear there'd be another palace built like it in any part of the country,' says he.

'Well, I'll stop that very soon, and you'll get the tool,' says she.

They called the lord's son up. 'The tool's up here in a big chest,' says she. 'Come up and reach it,' says she. 'It's very deep down in the chest, and I can't reach it.'

When the lord's son went up, he was reaching down for the tool in the chest,' and didn't she tip him in the chest and stuck the lid on him. 'I'll give you fresh air now and again,' says she, 'and you'll wait there until my ould man lands home.'

The account was sent back to the lord that the son was held there until her old man i'd be landed home. There was an express train chosen out for him and an express boat too until the poor ould Gobán landed in to them one evening, and they're at their supper. There was a body guard right along with Gobán to accompany the lord's son back again to wherever the castle was being built.

That castle might be Buckingham Palace that's now in it.[5]

༺༻

How Young Gobán's Wife Takes Her Revenge

Gobán's young son followed in his father's trade and became a builder in his own way. He settled down, got married and had a family. One day while young Gobán was working away, he was killed by a group of woodsmen.

In those days there was no saw to cut trees down. Trees were felled by cracking them and then splitting them. The wife of young Gobán knew very well the group of woodsmen that had killed her husband, and she developed a plan. One day she dressed herself up like a lady. She knew where these men were working in the woods, and she went to have her revenge for her husband. She went off to the woods where these men were cutting down timber. They had the trunk of an oak tree down, and their wedges already stuck in it. She approached them and spoke to them.

'I know a better way for ye to open that stick than that way,' says she. 'Why don't ye get six of ye on each side,' says she, 'and pull at it in yer best, and I'll hit at it with the wedge and then ye'll give me yer all for pulling.'

When they were all pulling at their best, she struck a side blow on the wedge. The wedge flew up and the tree trunk closed in on them, and the twelve men was caught with their fingers caught in the crack of the tree. She ditched the hatchet then and walked away.

'Revenge,' says she, 'for yer killing me young Gobán.' She cut the heads of the twelve men and left their hands stuck in the tree.

That's a woman that had the blood in her and walked off home to her family. She was a good woman.[6]

Curse on Lord Waterford's Family

Lord Waterford owned much property in his various estates, and he kept a gamekeeper to watch out for poachers. Now, there was a poor widow's son that used to poach on the Waterford estate and bring the catch back to his mother for her to eat.

Once the gamekeeper of Waterford saw this man with a rabbit, but they didn't catch him. They made out it was the widow's son as he had poached before. The boy was arrested, brought to trial, found guilty and was to be sentenced to be hanged by Waterford. His mother begged on her bare knees, bent on his doorstep to spare her son. She said he wasn't there at all that night because she had sent him to do something for her, but Waterford didn't heed her, and he got hanged.

Later his mother came to Waterford's house, went down on her knees on the doorstep and cursed him and prayed that he and all his descendants would meet with a sudden and improvident death. Since that day not one of the Beresford family has died a natural death once they had assumed the title of Waterford.

Soon after the hanging of the boy, Waterford closed down a well on his estate, which had been used regularly by the tenants for their water supply. He filled the well in with stones. Shortly after that, he took ill with drinking diabetes. He had to be placed by a window looking out at his lake. He couldn't get enough water to drink. As he was looking over his lake outside, he was shouting and roaring for 'Water, more water.' While sitting there one day, the well burst up, and the stones and concrete flowed down uncurbed whilst the tyrant was dying of thirst.

Since that time not one of the Waterford family has died a natural death. One Christmas Eve in the 1930s, one of them was found drowned near the kennels in eighteen inches of water in a little drain. The result has been that the presumptive heir to the Waterford title is always frightened of his life on assuming the title.[7]

Brother Frolie and Brother Peter

One time Brother Frolie landed up around the corner of a public house, and didn't he see a gentleman at the gate of the house when he went around it and saluted him.

'Good day, sir,' says Br Frolie.

'Good day,' says the gentleman answering him back. 'And what's your name?'

'My name is Brother Frolie,' says he, 'and what's your name?'

'My name is Brother Peter,' says he.

Didn't the two of them stick together and travel on the road for a while.

'What's your occupation?' says Br Frolie.

'I'm a fairy doctor,' says Br Peter, 'that can bring the dead to life and the live to dead.'

'Very well,' says Br Frolie, 'you're a very useful man to be with, you are.'

They ventured off together on the road and reached in to a city, where they saw there was black mourning in every corner in every street in the city. They asked what was the cause of the black mourning, and they up and told them that it was the king's daughter that was dead in the city. Didn't they set off, the two of them, until they landed at the king's palace. When they landed at the hall door, they rung the bell outside. The porter opened the door and saw the two gentlemen at the door outside.

'We're two doctors,' said Br Peter, and we heard that the king's daughter is dead here in the palace.

'Ah, Yes,' says the porter, 'she is dead, but what can you do for her,' he says.

'We're two doctors,' says Br Peter, 'that can bring the dead to life.'

As soon as the porter brought the account in to the king, they were admitted at once to sit in the waiting room within where his majesty was. They up and told him their occupation. The next thing, they were admitted in to the room where the daughter's remains was laid out.

When they landed in and examined the remains, Br Peter ordered a warm bath. 'While there's life, there's hope,' says he. The warm bath was landed in to the room where the poor daughter was laid out. Br Peter went to her head, and Br Frolie took her by the feet and laid her out over the warm bath. Br Peter went to go at his practice. Suddenly, the daughter stuck out her two hands and let a shout out of her.

'Ah, why?' says she.

When they heard her brought back to life, she having been laid out, as weak as ever, they moved her out in to the palace to her room where she belonged. The two doctors came in after her. The king and his wife and the whole court were near kissing the doctors. They were eating and drinking there for twenty-four hours. When they were leaving the following day, the king asked them what was their charge for their service?

'Nothing,' says Br Peter.

'Nothing,' says Br Frolie.

'That's too bad,' says the king, 'anything in the world?'

'Oh, nothing this time,' says Br Peter.

The king saw that Br Frolie was pulling at Br Peter.

'Oh, I see,' says the king, 'that your comrade wants you to take something for your service.'

'Well, I'll tell you,' says Br Frolie, 'you can give us a fat lamb.'

After that the two of them set out on the road once again, and didn't Br Peter place the live lamb on Br Frolie's back, and the lamb kicking and wriggling on him. When they were a while on the road, Br Frolie said he was getting tired carrying the lamb and asked Br Peter if he would carry the lamb for a bit.

'Indeed, I will not,' says Br Peter. 'I don't want the lamb. I want nothing.'

'Oh, sorra, what I'll do?' says Br Frolie.

After a while, they landed up where there was three roads met, and didn't they decide to go inside in a corner of a field to a tree, and Br Peter suggested killing the lamb. Now, Br Frolie says, 'I won't kill him.'

Br Peter had a fire set up and a pot got and went on to kill the lamb. When the lamb was skinned, cleaned and prepared, he put the lamb in to their pots. When they were boiling, Br Peter walked away for a walk around and left Br Frolie finishing the cooking of the lamb. As soon as he thought it was near boiled, stirring it to see if it was near boiled, what came wriggling up but the lamb's heart. Br Frolie pulled up the heart and gobbled in to it, eating it. Not long after he had eaten the lamb's heart, who'd landed back in but Br Peter.

'Take him up now, he's boiled enough,' says Br Peter. There was dishes and clothes, and all laid out for the lamb.

Br Frolie sat eating, and said to Br Peter, 'Why are you not bothering to eat the lamb?' asks Br Frolie.

'I'll eat only a bit of the lamb's heart,' says Br Peter, 'on the road.'

'Oh, a lamb has no heart,' says Br Frolie.

'Oh, well, if he hasn't a heart,' says Br Peter, 'you can eat the lamb altogether.'

When they had finished the meal, Br Frolie packed up but kept a bit of the lamb to eat on the road. They took to the road again without a farthing in their pocket. After some time, didn't they land in to another city and didn't they find that there was another king's daughter given up for dead.

The two of them then landed up to the hall door of the king's house and rang the bell. The king's porter asked them what they wanted.

'We're two head doctors that can cure the dead daughter.'

They were both invited in, shown to the daughter as she was laid out, and they ordered the bath.

'She'll be alright,' says Br Frolie, 'when she shakes her hands.'

Not long after the two of them had handled the bath and the other matters, the daughter recovered, and the king was overjoyed and asked them whatever they wanted, the king would serve up.

'Give him a bag of gold,' says Br Peter at last. Didn't the king serve up a nice leather bag filled with gold. Everyone in the king's family and palace thanked them, and they set out on the road again. Br Peter placed the bag of gold on Br Frolie's back.

After a while Br Frolie says, 'You'd better carry it a bit for now as I'm getting tired.'

'Carry it yerself,' says Br Peter. They went on travelling for a while, but when Br Peter knew Br Frolie was getting tired, they went in to the corner of a field and decided to lighten the load by dividing up the gold.

In three minutes, Br Peter had a big white sheepskin spread out on the grass and started to divide the money. Didn't he make three divisions of the money on the sheepskin.

'What are the three divisions for?' says Br Frolie to him.

'I've decided one for God, another division for the one who ate the lamb's heart.'

'Oh, that's me,' says Br Frolie. The money forced him to tell the truth.

'Take this portion of the gold now,' Br Peter says. He turned it over to him and bid him goodbye. 'I'm finished with you,' says he. 'Mind your money now.'

Br Frolie went along the road for a while 'til he spent his last penny of the bag of gold. Then he came to another city and didn't he hear that there was another death of a king's daughter there. He landed up to the king's palace, knocked on the hall door, and said he was the head doctor who could save the king's daughter. The porter told the king, and he was allowed in to help. He asked for the daughter's body to be brought to him and for a bath to be drawn. Then, he raised her over the warm bath. He gave her an old rub up and down and saying the words that he thought he remembered that Br Peter had said the last few times. He wasn't long working on the case 'til he saw the room getting very dark, and when he looked around who in the hangment did he see beside him but Br Peter.

'Well,' says Br Peter, 'you're an awful chancer, and you could be beheaded on the following day if this case fails on you.'

It was clear that Br Frolie needed Br Peter's help. As soon as Br Peter had finished his practice, he disappeared. Br Frolie had the daughter back to life, brought her out to the king and his family, and they all set to eating and drinking with the king's family. The king asked him what he wanted, and he got as much gold as he could carry, and he went off again.[8]

Carved head, Kilteel Abbey, Co. Kildare, 1975.

CHAPTER 4

Religious Tales and Legends

⌇⌇⌇

The Man That Went to Church for His Cow

ABOUT THE TIME OF THE Famine, there was a man named Mickey in the parish of Louisburgh, and he had a cow. He used to herd her on the roadside most of the time. One day the local minister met him and started talking with him.

'Don't you have any grass for the cow?' asks the minister.

'Hardly any,' Mickey replies.

'Well, you can put your cow in to the glebe land below the church, if you'd like,' says the minister.

The man was absolutely delighted. He drove his cow down to the glebe each day so she could graze there. After the fourth day, he met the minister again, and the minister says to him:

'Michael, you must come to my church on Sundays, otherwise I cannot give you the grass for your cow any longer.'

'Oh, alright, your Reverend,' says Mickey and went home.

On the following Sunday, he was up early and went to first Mass in the chapel, went home, had his breakfast and went down to church to the minister. That went on for a good few weeks. Then, somebody complained to the minister that Mickey was going to Mass every Sunday before he came to the Protestant church. The minister says, 'That couldn't be possible because I seen him here each Sunday myself.'

But the man persisted, and says to the minister, 'I'll prove to you that he's going to Mass, and if you stand with me at such a corner early next Sunday, you'll see him coming out from the chapel.'

The minister did so and indeed saw Mickey coming out from early Mass. He went over and spoke to Mickey, and says, 'Michael, did you not tell me that you'd come to my church?'

'I did,' says Mickey.

'And now I see you coming from the chapel,' says the minister. 'Can you explain your conduct?'

'Oh. Yes, Reverend,' said Mickey. 'I go to the chapel for the good of my soul; then I go to your church for the grass of the cow.'[1]

꙾

St Patrick Recreates a Bull

A long time ago, the people were building the chapel in Aghagower, and St Patrick got it built. All he had to do was only crack his fingers and all the people from the country round were there to help. When they were there, St Patrick had to provide food to feed them, and that was no easy task. Now, it turns out that he was a bit short of meat for them this one time, and he needed to get more food. There was a big rich man living near the place. St Patrick sent one of his men to him to ask him for some beef to help feed his men building the chapel. Didn't the rich man refuse him. Now, when St Patrick was told that the rich man had a mad bull down in a field nearby, he told one of his men to go down and take this bull back with him. The man went down and returned and told St Patrick that everyone working around there knew that this bull was mad and that no man could go in to the field and take him. St Patrick understood and gave the man his rod and says, 'Here, take this rod in your hand and go down and drive up the bull and have him killed.'

The man went down to the bull in the field and drove up the bull before him without any problem. The bull was killed, skinned, dressed and prepared to be cooked. Now, the fire was ready for the men were anxious to eat a bit of meat. The bull was hung on a spit – by three legs – and the fire underneath and all round. When the bull was ready for cutting, St Patrick came around.

'You can use all the meat,' says he, 'but save all the bones. Don't let one bit of a bone go to loss for I want them all back.'

The men ate the bull. They might have had a couple of days eating him. Now, when the ould rich feller that gave St Patrick the bull thought the bull was finished up, he came and demanded his bull back or the price of him from St Patrick. St Patrick told one of his men, 'Throw the bones into the hide.' He kneeled down, and he blew into the hide and up jumps the bull. St Patrick called the rich man and told him to put the bull in his field from where he was brought out. No man could go in to that field at all because of the bull. The rich man and all his household was converted in to the true name.[2]

The Cure of the Blind Girl

Stations were usually held twice a year in rural communities, and they were occasions when the local people assembled, prayed and were fed by the house chosen. It was the custom that holding the station was passed around within the community as it was a great honour and a burden for a family, especially a poor family.

One time the people out by Kilgeever, near Louisburgh, were holding a station through the night in one of the houses there. The station would last the whole night. The local custom was to pray all night and to leave Kilgeever in time to be at Mass either in Lecanvey or Killeen.

On this particular night there was a blind girl and her mother praying at the station. Late on this night, the people saw the priest riding on a horse up on the brow of the hill beyond the village as if he had been coming from the town, and they said, as he was going round the top of the graveyard, 'It's a good job we're saying the rosary, so he won't have to say it when he comes, and we'll continue on saying the five decades until he comes in.' The priest never put in an appearance at all.

Suddenly there was a streak of blue lightning, and it came straight down from the sky and reflected blue on all the faces all around the station. It hit on the rock where's the track of St Patrick's Knee, just opposite the holy well, and splashed blue light all around so that everyone could see everything plainly.

Right after the blue light shone, the blind girl began to shout, 'I can see. I can see.' She caught hold of people saying, 'I can see your face. There's your nose.' They all went down on their knees and prayed until daylight came. The young girl and her mother walked home along the road telling everyone they met about the miracle that had happened. Some of the people there said that she should have stayed, but she wanted to spread the word.

There was one man in that crowd that couldn't see what had happened, and he went around saying, in a pitiful way, 'Where was it?' and 'What was it? I didn't see it.'[3]

❦

Saint Martin Sends a Supper

St Martin's Day on the 11th of November is a festival day to celebrate St Martin, and on that day, people used kill a goose as part of the celebration.

Now, once there was a man and his wife who lived in Carrowmore but down towards the sea, and they were very poor. On this particular night, the wife had told the man that she would go out and see if she could get a little help with food from some of her friends and neighbours. The husband was left sitting by himself by the fire in their house. He was feeling sad and lonely having nothing to eat. He decided to go on a walk to the other end of the village to a house he knew there and visited with them for a while talking away. The people of the house were cooking a goose that night, and they asked him if he wanted to have the supper with them, but he was so shy of his poorness that he wouldn't stay to eat or remain there, and so he went home.

As he approached the window of his own house, he noticed there was a light shining within, and he said to himself that the wife must have returned. He entered the house and found a fine fire going, a candle lit in the window, and a good supply of food cooked and left on the table. He called his wife thinking she was in some other part of the house, and had found food for them to eat, but he heard no reply. He sat down and ate a good supper and thanked St Martin for earlier in the night, he had asked him to send some help.[4]

The Devil Woman That Tempted John Mulhearn

John Mulhearn of Durrycoosh, near Raheens on the Kilmeena road, was a carter, and he used to arrange the carting of porter and corn from the around the area, the midlands and even as far away as Dublin. He was well known to cart corn to one of the Newport mills and to the Livingstones brewery of Westport. John would be up before the crack of dawn with only the light of the moon. He didn't need a watch or a clock, and indeed no one had them in those days save maybe a priest or a doctor.

One time he was on his journey going with his empty cart to pick up a load in Ballina. Suddenly, this woman jumped in beside him in the cart. She was good-looking and very interesting in the way she talked to him. She was shoving in on him on the seat tight like, and just then, a priest comes and jumps in to the cart. The priest knew very well that was a colleen that had disappeared. John bid the priest welcome.

The priest says to him, 'Do you not know me?'

'No, I don't,' says John.

'Well, I'm the priest that baptised you, and that woman,' he says, 'is the devil, and I've come to save you for you'd be in danger of judgement in another hour.'

When John understood what had happened, he realised he could have died.

Now John noticed that there was a cart opening in the wall on one side of the road as he was driving along. The priest told him to pull in there and to keep the cart off the road. Next thing he seen was a naked man running as hard as the breeze could go and two hounds after him.

'They are the madaí allta,' (wild hounds) says the priest, 'and if the man makes it to the burying ground up above before the hounds catch him, he'll be safe for the Judgement Day, but if they catch up on him, he's gone.'

The priest asks, 'Do you know that man?'

'I think I do,' says John. 'He's a neighbour of mine, and he's been complaining for a long time.'

'Well, he died just now,' says the priest. 'So, pull out now and go your way and don't be out again before daylight. Remember I'm here because I baptised you, and I have a special interest in your soul.'

When John was coming back that same road the next day, there was no cart way or breach in the wall at all.[5]

The Tinker That Bested Death and the Devil

At the time of the bad times here in the Famine years, there was a poor tinker, a tin-smith, and he said to his wife, 'One day, Mary,' says he, 'I'm going to try my fortune in some other part of the country before we starve here.'

He took his leather pouch budget and packed up, and he set out for the road and faced the country before him. As he was passing through a big mire, that's a drowning place on a mountain, didn't he get stuck in to a big dike, a big drain, and the devil a man, the poor fellow, was getting him out of it, as handy as he thought. Didn't he begin roaring and yelling.

'What in the world will I do?' says he. 'I cannot get out of the dike.'

Wasn't it with great laughter a fine gentleman landed on the bank of the dike looking down over him.

'What in the hangment are you doing there?' says he to him.

'I cannot get out of the dike, sir,' says the tinker to him.

'What would you give the man that would release you out of it?' says the gent.

'Anything in the world that you want,' says he, 'but pull me out of it.'

'Will you give me your soul?' says the gent to him.

'I will, and welcome,' says he. He promised his soul to him and wrote it down for him, then and there.

When the tinker was freed, he set off through the country, the poor fellow, and was thinking how would he manage with the gentleman he had given his soul to until he spent his twelve months gone from Mary, his wife. At the end of the twelve months, he says, 'I'll return home to see how is my wife and garsúns', and he had travelled the County Galway, nearly all over, by the end of the twelve months.

Now on his journey coming home, didn't he meet a poor beggarman on the road, and didn't the beggarman up and ask alms of him.

'Well, all the alms I have got left after my long twelve months is only three shillings today,' says he, 'and I'll give you one shilling of them,' handing one shilling to the poor beggar.

Then didn't he go along the road, and soon he met another beggar, and the poor fellow was roaring out for alms. Well, the tinker turned over and gave him the second shilling to the second beggar. And he hadn't gone on long until didn't he meet a third beggar, and didn't he give him the third shilling. He still had a cross belonging to him, and he was beginning to cry about what would Mary and the garsúns do when he got home as he had nothing at all to give them.

After that, didn't he meet a fourth man. After he had finished up, he hadn't even a cross.

'You're on your journey,' the beggar says.

'I am,' says he, 'I am bound for home.'

'Do you want to get a favour from a friend?' says the beggar.

'I do,' says he, 'want a favour, if I can get it that will help me.'

'I'm going to best three requests on you,' says the beggar. 'Whatever requests you'll ask,' he says, 'you'll get them.'

'I have a chest in the house,' says he, and 'I'd like to get it full with meal every day of the year.'

'That you must get,' says the beggar. 'The next request you'll get it too,' he says.

'I want anything that'll get in to my budget,' says he, 'not to leave it 'til I give it leave.'

'That you must get,' says the beggar.

'And lastly, I have an apple tree growing at my house that produces a lot of apples in the year,' says he, 'and anybody that will meddle with it will be stuck to it 'til I'll get him out of it.'

'That you must get,' says the beggar.

So the tinker parted from the beggar, took up his budget, stuck it on his back and set off on the road for home. Now as he was travelling along he came to the dike where he was the twelve months before. Who in the hangment did he see standing at the brink of the dike but the buck that pulled him out of it.

'Well,' says the buck, 'are you ready now for coming along with me?'

'I am,' says the tinker. 'Now didn't I hear that you could make a hound and a hare?' said he to him.

'I can,' said the gentleman.

'Well, let us see you let them out and make them run,' says the tinker.

It wasn't long 'til out goes the hare, and off go brách with the hound after it. The poor tinker had his eyes stuck watching the race, and the hunt, the hare and the hound. What did the tinker do but to open the lid of his budget, and the hound was so close up to the hare and in pops the hare in the budget to him and in goes the hound after it to collar the hare within in the budget. Then he clapped the lid on them.

'Wait here, now,' says the tinker turning the key on it. He sees no more of the buck; he had him in the budget then.

Again, the tinker stuck his budget up on his back and didn't he hear the noises and howls of all of them within. 'Be quiet there,' he says, giving it an odd hit over his shoulder. He was travelling along on the road until he came on a crossroads, and he saw two men threshing corn on the road. Didn't he take down the budget from his back.

'Come,' he says to the threshers, 'won't you give my budget a couple of blows of your flails; it's bloody hard on me back.'

'Alright,' says they, 'leave it down.' As soon as he left it down, didn't the buck within let out one big roar, and the two thresher men set off like blazes when the roar was let, and he saw no more of them, and the tinker just continued on.

The tinker threw the budget up on his shoulder again, and the buck within felt every hit on him over his shoulder within the box. He struck it from time to time on his back on his journey making for home until he landed into a village. When he heard there was a blacksmith within his forge and he hammering away, he threw down the budget from his shoulder and told the blacksmith to give it a crack.

'Alright,' says the blacksmith, spitting on his hands and taking up the hammer. 'Leave it down.' He gave it one crack, and a roar was let from within in. The first crack he gave it, the roar was let out, and off go brách with the blacksmith out of his forge with the fright that was taken out of him when the roar was let out.

The tinker landed the budget back on his shoulder and set off for home and didn't stop 'til he landed up at the wife, at Mary. As soon as he landed in, of course, Mary ran to embrace him, to kiss him for she hadn't seen him for twelve months.

'Rise, Mary,' he says, 'and get a bit to eat for me,' says he.

'How can 1 get you a bit to eat,' says she, 'when 1 haven't a bit inside the chest?'

'Put down the pot there,' he says, 'and go up and make a bit of stirabout for us. Go up to the chest for meal.'

'How can I go to the chest,' says she, 'when there's only cobwebs in it since you went?'

'So, I'll go up,' says he, 'and get the meal meself.'

'Alright,' says she. When he raised the lid of the chest, wasn't it full up with meal.

'Come up, Mary,' says he, 'you were telling me ye had no meal.' So, Mary ran up to the room when she heard the words of the husband above.

'Oh, Lord dear,' says she, 'what in the world put the meal in it? Myself and the garsúns are starved since you went begging,' she says. Then he took his budget and landed it above within the chimney in the room. Now and again, he used to go up and have a look at the budget and wasn't the buck inside with every roar out of him asking to be let out.

'Wait there,' says he, and he kept him there for seven years. At the end of the seven years, he went up to see his ould mate that pulled him out of the dike. At the end of the seven years, he roared at him that he didn't want his soul at all 'til he got rid of him. So he bid his goodbye to his ould mate that pulled him out of the dike.

Now the tinker was living as happy as could be until he got to be a right old man. So didn't Death land up one morning to his front door and knock on it.

'I have just come for you,' he says to the tinker.

'Have you?' says he. 'And who are you?' says he to him.

'I'm Death,' says he.

'Come in so,' says the tinker, 'and sit down until I'm ready.'

So, Death came in, but where did he put him sitting but quickly opened the mouth of the budget. He gave him one thrust in and closed the lid on him, and he held him there for seven years. There

RELIGIOUS TALES AND LEGENDS

wasn't one person dying around the country for the seven years. At the end of the seven years, didn't Death let a roar out within the budget asking to let him loose.

'Let me out of the budget,' he says. 'I'll do anything for ye ye want.'

'Would you make a head doctor of me?" says the tinker.

'Alright,' says the Devil.

So, the tinker opened the budget, and let the Death ladeen with the thin legs go.

'But remember,' says the tinker, 'anywhere you see me as the head doctor,' he says, 'don't meddle with it to cure the patient.' So, the tinker was off curing all before him all over the country. One day he landed up to a certain place where a death was near given up. Didn't he see Death above at the head of the patient. Didn't he take the patient and switch him around on the bed so Death would be around where the feet were. The next morning early enough who was outside but Death.

'Didn't I think I was done with you,' says the tinker.

'Why did you move the patient down to where his feet was when he was dying?'

'Faith, I was short of money,' he says, 'and I wanted to help save my patient. Come in,' says he, 'and sit down.'

'Oh, no fear,' says the Devil, 'of me coming in again. I got my fill of you the last time.'

'Then wait,' says he, 'until I'm ready. I have something to say to the poor wife.' Out he set, and himself and Death were travelling the laneen to his home.

As the tinker was approaching his house, he says, 'Wait. I'd like to bring in an apple. Would you ever go to that apple tree outside the door in the garden and pick me an apple.

'I'll go down,' says Death, 'and get the apple for you.'

Death goes in to the garden and reaches for the apple, and the first moment he put his hand up to catch the apple, wasn't he stuck to the tree.

'What's delaying you?' says the tinker to him.

'I'm stuck to the tree,' says he. 'I can't get away.'

'Wait there,' says the tinker, 'wait there.'

'For goodness sake,' says he, 'let me go. I'll never bother with you again until you'll want to go yourself.'

The tinker turned back in to his house and left the poor fellow sticking to the tree outside.

'I'll make head doctor of ye for head and feet,' says Death, 'but just let me go.'

So, the tinker let him go, and instead of being a tinker, he was a head doctor all over the country. He was wandering away until he got to be a grey ould maneen, 'til he craved Death to come and take him away for he got to be a weathered little maneen. Death landed up and took him away with him, landed up to the gates of heaven to St Peter.

'I cannot let you in,' says St Peter to him, 'when you got your three requests, you didn't ask for Heaven. I'm the angel that came before you that you gave alms to that has given you the privilege you have got to talk to me.'

'Well, St Peter, if you don't let me in,' says he, 'I'll have a try at the other fellow.'

So, the tinker landed up to the gates of Hell. One of the porters landed up to the gate to him.

'What do you want?' says the porter.

'I want to get in here,' says the tinker.

'Well, I need to see the head boss about that,' says the porter.

'Who are you?'

He told him he was the tinker. The porter went back, and he told the head boss who it was that was at the gates.

'Oh, for goodness sake,' says the head boss, 'get him away altogether from the gates. I spent seven years within in his old budget, and that's enough with him. Bring him up to that nice houseen built at the crossroads between Hell and Heaven, let him stay there 'til the end of time.'[6]

Holy Water in the Churn

Me grandmother, Nelly Ó Máille of Glenkeen, near Louisburgh, had seven or eight milkers and usen't have a bit of butter in her churn. From time to time one of the priests would spend the night in her house before saying a Mass in the morning or making a visit. She was greatly concerned that she wouldn't have any butter for the priest. So, she up and told the priest when he went out to Bundorragha.

'I've seven or eight milkers,' she says to the priest, 'and isn't it a poor case that I have no butter to show, Father?' Says she, 'I'm sorry I haven't a bit of butter to leave down for your breakfast.'

'Why, Nelly,' says he to her like that, 'you haven't any butter? I'll tell you what you'll do, Mrs Ó Máille,' he says. 'When you're making your churning, sprinkle some holy water in it three times,' he says.

Nelly did so, and thanks be to God her churn was full of butter the next churning she made. She used to bring three hundred weight of crock butter into Westport after that, and she used to get a penny a pound more than any other that was coming to the stores.[7]

Bringing in the potatoes, Burrishoole Lodge, Newport, Co. Mayo, 1943.

CHAPTER 5

Historical Tradition

༄

The Borrowed Congregation

AT ONE TIME THE PROTESTANT minister in Louisburgh, Reverend Seymour, was going to be removed elsewhere because his congregation was too small. It seems that himself and the parish priest, Father Pat Gibbons, were quite friendly and used often meet and walk as far as the sea. One day the minister says to him, 'This 'ill be the last time we'll walk together because the bishop is coming down to examine the congregation on Sunday, and I haven't much of a congregation left, only a few.'

The priest says, 'I'll send down some of my flock if you are agreeable.'

On the next Sunday came, when the people came into the old chapel for Mass, the priest came round, and he called out some of the men he had selected, including McEvilly, Durcan and others, and told them to go down and sit in the pews of the Protestant church. This was before Mass. They went down after Mass and filled up the pews.

At the end of his visit, the bishop says to the minister, 'Upon my honour, I have never seen a finer congregation,' and so the minister was left in place, and the bishop went off satisfied with all he had seen.

There were only a few Protestants in the congregation at the time of Fr Gibbons.[1]

༄

Thomas Fights O'Donnell Over Wrack

Thomas an Oiláin, the islander, was a soldier and came to live in Caher, near Louisburgh, and later moved to Dadreen, above the Killaries. While he was in Caher, he lived in the same house with a fellow soldier, Dogherty.

Now, there was a fellow named O'Donnell that lived at the three crossroads on the way down to the sea in Carrowmore. He was a real bully and a devil. If a farmer went down to the shore to pick a load of wrack or seaweed, O'Donnell would insist that the man had to throw in a horse load of wrack on to his land wherever he asked. Wrack was used by spreading it on the land to help improve the land and the crops.

Dogherty and Thomas were new to the Carrowmore area and didn't know anything about O'Donnell's rule. One spring morning, Dogherty went down to the shore to get a load of wrack for his farm. On his return to his home, he was challenged by O'Donnell, and he demanded that Dogherty should deliver his first load in to his farm.

'This is the first load of wrack I have ever brought up,' says Dogherty, 'and if I throw this load to you, I'll be too late for my breakfast if I have to go back to the sea to get another load as I don't like going home empty, but let me take this load home, and I'll promise you, you can have the next.'

O'Donnell agreed. 'Go ahead,' says he.

Dogherty went home, and his breakfast was there and ready for him. Now, Dogherty had to think of a plan so that he would not have to deliver the second load to O'Donnell as he had promised.

'I don't feel well at all,' says Dogherty to Thomas, 'but I'll just stretch out on the bed for a while to get some rest and try to recover. Would you go down for the next load of wrack, and I might feel better by the time you get back.'

Thomas took the same horse and cart and went down to the shore for the load of wrack. When he was coming along home, O'Donnell came out from his house.

'Where the hell are you going?' says O'Donnell. 'Why don't you throw in to my place your load of wrack as you know you should?'

'Why should I throw my wrack in there? Isn't it home to my own land I'm bringing it?'

'I'll take no more nonsense from you,' says O'Donnell. 'You know right well you have to throw that load of wrack in here.'

'There's one thing I know for sure,' says Thomas, 'and that's not one stalk of my wrack will ever go inside your fence.'

'Then you'll fight for it?' says O'Donnell.

'Why certainly, if necessary,' says Thomas.

The two men fought, and the bully O'Donnell was beaten. From that day on, no one in Carrowmore ever had to throw a load of wrack in to O'Donnell's farm, and O'Donnell had to take care to gather in his own wrack.[2]

The Flogging of Brian MacNamara

Two brothers, Brian or Breeneen MacNamara and his younger brother, were arrested for sheep stealing round Louisburgh. During the trial, sufficient evidence was produced that the charge was proven against both brothers, and the jury voted for it. The brothers were sentenced by the judge to be flogged from the bridge to the end of Long Street in Louisburgh, while tied to the tail of a cart, and a soldier on each side of the cart.

The older brother, Brian, was the leader, and he was flogged first. When they had finished with him, he said, 'Since I'm already stripped, I'll take my brother's share, and you can spare him the flogging as he's weak.'

The man in charge denied his request, and said it was not in order for him to make such a request and that the younger brother would have to be flogged separately. As they were flogging him, he fell unconscious under the cart, but he was picked up by the soldiers, and they flogged him again until the end of the journey.

Now, the brothers were released after the flogging, and they were exhausted, but they immediately got to planning their revenge. It's on the official record that on the very night they had been flogged, they went out later and stole some more sheep.

When the police caught them the second time, they drove them through the streets of Louisburgh with a sheep's head tied around each of their necks. They were tried again, found guilty and sentenced to transportation to Van Diemen's Land in Tasmania. There's a good lot of their MacNamara descendants out there in Australia.

In those days there were plenty of men from the west of Louisburgh who were arrested for sheep stealing and transported to Australia.[3]

⤳

The Man with the Thin Skull

It was not uncommon that faction fights would break out between certain loosely organised groups in the countryside. They happened around the Louisburgh area where there were faction fights between the Gallinacks and Granastones at Tooreen. One of these fights, with both sides using sticks, went on for a good while. Some of the wives had even concealed their sticks under their coats when they were walking along. In one particular fight, a man was knocked out by a crack of a stick on the head. He recovered a little but later died. The police arrested a good number of the participants and were able to identify one man to be charged with the killing.

The assailant was prosecuted on a charge of murder. In his defence he managed to get the services of a very clever lawyer. The lawyer asked the judge for and was granted an exhumation order to exhume the victim in order to have his skull examined by an expert authority. The expert was at the trial court and swore that he had nothing against the deceased man, but he argued that the man's skull was abnormally thin and that it would have taken very little force to break it. The expert noted that the crack of the stick in the fight would not have been a particularly heavy one.

The judge says to the accused, 'What have you to say for yourself in defence?'

'Well, Your Worship, I'll just ask you this one question,' he says, 'what business had a man with a thin skull like that being in a faction fight at all?'

The judge looked at him. 'Well,' he says, 'if indeed he had a thin skull, then he had no business at all being involved in a faction fight.'

The case was dismissed.[4]

Johnny Durcan, the Swindler

Johnny Durcan lived alone in Roonashionach in Askillaun, near the road from Louisburgh to Roonah, and wanted to get married. He went about making inquiries and found there were two young women who might be available. In those days, it was the custom that the woman would bring a dowry with her at the time of the wedding, but that it would be paid beforehand.

Now, Durcan was a bit of a chancer, and he took a dowry from each of the two girls for to get married to them. He promised each of them he'd marry her. It turned out that the two girls ended up knowing each other, and they exchanged their stories. To help them know what best to do, they went to the priest and told the priest of Durcan getting away with £5 from each of them. The priest asked Durcan to come before him, and simple conniving Durcan says, 'Why can't I marry the two of them, Father?'

'How could you marry the two of them?' says the priest.

'Well, if not then, what'll I do?' says he.

'I don't know what you'll do,' says the priest.

Durcan kept the £10 he had swindled from the girls and went off to England. When he landed up in England, he had the luck to get into service with a well-known doctor. Durcan was a fine good-looking fellow, and the doctor's wife fell in love with him or at least she liked him very much. She had a plan how to finish off her husband, and he was supportive. She and your man gave the ould buck doctor a slow dose that couldn't be noticed. Durcan used to be out in the field pulling herbs every day for medicines, such as hart's tongue and dandelion, and the like. The ould doctor was declining every day for the next four months. They were giving him their poison real slow. By the end of six months, he pegged out.

Durcan then married the widow woman, and after a while he became known as Doctor Durcan for he had studied up well on his herbs. He stayed on there in the practice then and waited 'til the ould lady pegged out. Then, he sold the practice and set out for America and set up a great doctor's store in New York City with several branches around. He worked long and hard at the herbal business and after many years in it he was a millionaire near.

Durcan married again, and he decided to return to Mayo. He landed up in Louisburgh with two of the greatest ladies you could look at with their great golden bracelets hanging around them. One was his wife and the other was her sister. Everyone in

Louisburgh admired them. They spent many weeks touring about the coast where he was born and bred. Of course, he was called Dr Durcan by one and all around. He stayed for six months around Louisburgh, but then returned to America and went back to his business again. Sometime later, when he was working at his books counting his riches, didn't his foreman stick him with a dagger in the middle of the back, and that put an end to his swindling.[5]

The Poor Boy That Became a Doctor

There was a family by the name of Lavelle that lived in the village of Carrowmore, near Louisburgh. They were very poor and had six or seven children. The eldest was a boy, Edward, then about seventeen years.

One day Edward went off about his business, and he didn't turn up that night. A search was made for him the following day. No trace of him could be found that day nor on the following days. There was no tale or tidings heard of him, and he was given up for lost. Now, in those days it was more or less the custom for lads to stray off, and indeed even in my younger days. There was no work for the lads, and so some of them just walked about looking for some place better. Some would join the military, others would look for work in the cities.

At the end of seven years, the father and mother were one night lying in their bed, and a rap came to the door. The woman called to her husband. 'That's Edward's knock,' says she.

'Don't be foolish,' says he, 'it couldn't be.'

'Oh, it is,' says she, 'it's our own son's knock.'

They got up and opened the door quickly, and there was a well-dressed young man, wearing a Caroline Fedora hat, which was the vogue of the day. Who was there, but their long-lost son, Edward. One can imagine the surprise and joy of the family after his return. He told them his story, how he had wandered away getting a bit of food here and there, working for a day or a week if he could, always going on until he reached the city of Dublin. There he got into the service of a doctor that lived out in the country. The doctor was so well pleased with Edward's work that he took a great interest in him and helped get him educated. Finally, with the good doctor's help, he studied medicine, became a doctor and afterwards worked in the doctor's office. Then, the old doctor decided to go out to France, and he brought Edward along with him, and they remained there for several years. After that time, they returned to Ireland, and it was then that Edward decided to visit to his parents. Well, he gave them a good sum of money to relieve them of their poverty, but he then went away soon afterwards and was never heard of again.[6]

The Exploits of Lynchehaun

James Lynchehaun of Achill was a clerk for Mrs MacDonnell, and she lived in Achill. One time he was coming from Newport and was quite drunk. He went into her house and beat her badly. He took in some whin bushes or gorse and pushed them under her clothing and between her legs and bashed her around her eyes. The police were looking for him and were travelling through the mountains of Achill, Currane and Tiernaur. There's even the policeman who lost his life and died of hardship in those places. Westport hospital and Castlebar hospital was filled up with the poor policemen as they were kept out night and day looking for him.

The police were used to taking a man on suspicion merely because he was coming home late at night. Lynchehaun had lost the thumb of one of his hands, but they wouldn't bother looking for that mark when they stopped a man. They'd bring him in merely because of his size. Pat Mullarky of Gortawarla was often arrested for being him. He was of a similar size.

Now Lynchehaun was all the time in a dug out in his father's house in Achill, just under the fireplace, but he couldn't live there anymore. He was getting into bad health. There was a £200 reward for anyone that would give information to catch him. He said to his wife to give the information on him so as she'd have the money. She did, and the police captured him. When they were coming along with him towards Newport in a sidecar, the police – one on each side of him – and it was getting dark, he said he'd like a smoke and for them to loosen his handcuffs, and they did so. Now, there was a pond of water ahead with stepping-stones leading through it. When they took off the handcuffs, he cracked a match. It was night and when he jumped out from between them, he took to the stepping-stones and got away. Now, they had to start looking for him again.

The police caught him a second time. His trial went on, and Mrs MacDonnell swore against him, and he got life imprisonment and went to prison. His brother was a fish dealer in Dublin, and he used to supply his gaol with fish on every Friday. Lynchehaun was in touch with the brother, and he used to have a card hanging on his fish cart saying '£500 if you let the prisoner free,' but making no mention of what prisoner. One of the guards took a liking to the idea and took the money. The result was that Lynchehaun was able to escape. There was a fishing boat ready that used to supply the brother with fish. He escaped and made his tracks straight for the fishing boat as he knew where she was. The boat took off straight away and he landed up in Southampton. There was an American liner there going out, and he went aboard and got off to America.

When he got to New York, he had neither work nor money. He got work in an icehouse, and he and another fellow were loading the ice on the lorries. They were very heavy hunks of ice, and his partner says to him one morning:

'I'm going for a drink but say it's to the toilet I'm going if the boss comes round.'

When Lynchehaun was packing the lorry while his partner was gone, he would take his tongs and heave the heavy ice hunks in like they were bricks. His boss came along when he was loading.

'You'll hurt yerself, me man, heaving them heavy hunks,' he says. 'Where's your partner?'

Lynchehaun says, 'He's gone to the toilet.'

His boss says, 'Are you any kind of a scholar – can you write?'

'I'm a middling scholar,' he says, 'but what I'd write, you couldn't read.'

'Well then, son,' he says, 'will ye come with me.' He took him to his office and put him to write, and he couldn't read his writing, but he gave him a job in the office.

Later on, he went to Chicago, and he was taken in Chicago by the British police. The Hibernians there took him up and fought the case for him, and when he won the case, he was at liberty again.

The defence was that only a murderer could be brought back to Ireland for trial, but he hadn't actually murdered Mrs MacDonnell.

Next, he arrived in Cleveland, where there were many Irish working, and he got a job as a scab on the docks. Well, now, he was some years there, and he wrote home, and I don't know who, and made a bet that he would go back to Achill, get arrested and get away again. So, he did come home, and went in to his father's house while his mother was putting down a fire, and when she turned round, she says, 'James, in the name of God, is that you?'

There were some youngsters in the house, and he put his hand over her mouth and stopped her from saying any more.

The next day it was about three o'clock, and he walked out of the house and over to the schoolmaster's house which was close by. The schoolmaster and his teacher wife were at school. He went in to the house and pulled everything down on the floor and broke all that was in it. The servant girl ran out and told the policeman who was close by. The policeman came along and arrested him. On the way to the barracks, they met the schoolmaster and his wife, and the sergeant told the schoolmaster what he had done in his house. James gave his hat a little bit of a heave back.

'Oh, let him go,' says the schoolmaster, 'let him go. It's all right.' He had seen his forehead, and he knew who he was.

Lynchehaun was brought into Newport after his arrest, but he managed to escape again.

Now, when he was taking the train for Dublin, a policeman, who was going to Dublin, came in and sat down near him. They started talking about one thing and another until he mentioned the name of the Lynchehaun matter.

Lynchehaun says, 'It's a wonder that they never could catch him.'

'Well, if I was a policeman in them days, I'd have caught him,' and him riding the train with himself.

'I'm proud of your cleverness,' says Lynchehaun. 'Please give me your address.' He did, and so Lynchehaun wrote to him from America saying that he was the man he was riding beside on the train saying how he was going to catch him, and he gave him the copy of the conversation. So Lynchehaun won his £1,000 bet.

Then he went over to Liverpool and joined the police there. He found out that the English police had two warrants out for his own arrest, and he carried them in his own pocket. When the Great World War came along, he was in the army for a while.

After the war was over, he set himself up as a gangster in Liverpool, and he used to hold court on anyone that stole a car. He'd bring a woman up from the docks while his wife was at Mass, and when she'd come home, she'd find Lynchehaun in bed with her. She'd throw a shovel or anything she could find at him, and she'd pass a very severe sentence on him.[7]

❧

The Rebel Priests in Killadoon

After the 1798 Rebellion, two rebel priests, Father Maguire and Father Murphy, came all the way across Ireland from Wexford to Killadoon, just below Killeen. At that time Father Lyons was out at Killadoon. The two priests were on the run and staying there so they would not be caught. Killadoon was a small village of about one hundred houses in those days.

Irish history is riddled with spies, and there was one there in the village or around who had heard about the two priests arriving in the community, and he went in to Louisburgh to inform the guards on them. The yeomen came out to Killadoon, surrounded Fr Lyons' house, and went in to talk with him. The two priests, Fr Murphy and Fr Maguire, were hidden by Fr Lyons in a secret room in his house. The head yeoman asked Fr Lyons, 'Wasn't there two other priests here today saying Mass here above in the chapel?'

'No,' says Fr Lyons, 'because I wasn't able to read Mass today. I wasn't well at all.'

'Well,' says the head yeoman, 'we were informed by a reliable source who came in and told us.'

The head yeoman ordered his men to go out and bring in the informer as he intended to flog him or shoot him for bringing him out on such a wasted journey. The informer was found and brought back to the yeoman, and he was afraid for his life. Fr Lyons asked permission to speak with the informer alone, and he was allowed. After that talk, the informer admitted that he had made a mistake by informing, and he got a pardon from the priest. The head yeoman was especially annoyed at the turn of events as he felt that he was fighting for the established order in Ireland and wanted to root out any and all people who supported the rebels. He had the informed flogged but not shot.

Fr Lyons felt that when he took his vows for ordination, he didn't think that he would be having to be involved in these types of matters.[8]

The Stick That Beat a French Sword in 1798

After the time the French had landed at Killala and invaded Ballina in August 1798, they swept down in to Castlebar where they routed the British troops. The French regrouped in Castlebar and stayed there a while. At that time there was an old man, named Quinn, living in Breaghwy out the road from Castlebar. His son-in-law, who wasn't long married, had a fine young mare. One day he went to Castlebar with a bag of oats on the horse to sell. As he was coming in to the centre of town, one of the French officers came up to him and demanded the mare off him. The young man felt he was obliged to give up his mare to him. When he walked home without the mare and told the story, his father-in-law became excited and got into an awful bad temper at the idea of the mare being taken from his son-in-law.

'How will we get on without the mare or how are we going to live at all?' he asks the son-in-law. 'We might as well clear out of here for we have no business in it. In my day,' he says, 'I'd die before I'd let the mare go. As soon as the sun rises in the morning, you'll have to find the mare and bring her home or you'll not rest here anymore.'

On the next morning, the son-in-law told the ould man that he wouldn't go into Castlebar after the mare. Ould man Quinn was furious with him and decided to go in to Castlebar by himself with just his blackthorn stick, which he knew how to use well as a shillelagh. When he got to town, he approached one of the French officers and demanded his mare back. The officer only mocked him, and that made the ould man even more angry. He says, 'I'm going to get back my mare at all costs.'

'Well,' says the officer, 'are you willing to fight for her?'

'There isn't a good man that wouldn't fight with a stick for his mare,' says the ould man.

'Well,' says the officer, 'remember if you do fight, you're going to lose your life.'

'I'm as well to lose me life as lose me mare,' he replies.

The officer ordered one of his men to mount on horseback with his sword and be ready to fight the ould man standing there all alone on the street with only his blackthorn stick.

'Are you ready now?' asks the officer.

'I'm ready,' says the man. 'Let him come on.'

The French officer rode towards the ould man at full speed, making a fair wind brandishing his sword as he came. The ould man ducked avoiding the sword but swung his blackthorn stick catching the rider on the back of his head killing him instantly with the one blow.

The senior officer said the man was well entitled to his horse and gave him back his mare and off home he went with it.[9]

&c;

The Rebel Fay

Denis Browne of Westport House decided to name a new town in honour of his younger brother, Louis, who had been recently killed fighting with the British army in Canada. He started building the new town of Louisburgh in 1795 on the Bunowen River near the old village of Kilgeever.

After the Rebellion of 1798, Browne also undertook to build a Protestant church in Louisburgh, Saint Catherine's, to support the local Protestant community there. When the church was in the course of being erected, a man named Fay, who was said to be a native of Bofin, was employed as a mason. He was certainly a clever mason. When the church was nearly finished, Browne came to inspect the building and was accompanied by the usual cavalry, infantry, and a Protestant minister or canon, named Reverend Nicholson. The inspection turned out to be a big celebration for the event.

During the inspection, Browne found fault with the size of the church. The contractor put the blame on Fay for making it small. Browne upbraided Fay, and Fay said, 'The church is big enough. It would hold more Protestants than the kingdom of heaven.'

Browne asked who Fay was and where he came from, and being told he was a stranger from Bofin, he ordered him arrested. On hearing of that order, Fay ran for his lodging, and rushing in to the room where he slept, he took out his firelock muskets and pointed them at his pursuers. Having misfired twice, he threw them from his shoulder and made two halves of them on the wall. The girls of the house had wet the pair of his muskets for fun because Fay was well known to be a famous shot.

Fay then turned and ran away from the lodging. The soldiers fired volleys and immediately followed after him, but the land surrounding the village on towards Legan, just northeast of Louisburgh, was covered with underbrush and trees. There were trees then from Willy Durcan's house at Bunowen all the way to Old Head. It was wooded country with birch and brushwood. Fay escaped in the woods and hid there until he was able to be taken away with a boat going to Clifden and was never heard of again.

The soldiers and yeomen were in a rage at having seen Fay escape on them. They searched all the houses in Bunowen, and after finding a piece of a stick or handle of a pike in the thatch of an old house of William MacNicholas, they arrested poor William and took him as a prisoner to Louisburgh Square to have him shot. He was on his knees praying, and the squad were ready to fire, when the Protestant minister, Rev. Nicholson, intervened and got his pardon on condition that he would change his name to Nicholson, which he did. The MacNicholas of Bunowen were called Nicholsons ever after.

The soldiers were frustrated once again by this second missing of a killing. When they turned around, they saw a man coming in to Louisburgh over the bridge. The soldiers presented their firearms, aimed at the innocent man and riddled him. The man's name was Garvey from Knockeen, just near the Carrownisky River in Furmoyle. The villagers were so afraid of the soldiers, they did not approach poor dead Garvey until night came and the soldiers had gone away. It was common for the local people not to appear to be sympathetic to someone being shot by a landlord. The same thing happened in Newport in 1798 when Father Manus Sweeney was hung there, and the locals did not dare to cut him down from the temporary gallows until the evening.[10]

The Sack of Mount Browne

After the French invasion at Killala in '98, the French troops were joined by local men. Soon after the routing of the British troops when they fled after the Races of Castlebar, one of the French companies pursued Denis Browne and his militia from Castlebar to his house in Mount Browne, outside Westport on the Carrowbeg River. There Browne got backed up by a bit of the garrison at Mount Browne. He decided to make a stand for it against the French and dug a trench there. The French and the Irish dug a trench facing them on the side beyond the big house just three hundred and eighty yards from the Aghagower road. After a short period of fighting, the dead smelled so much that neither side could stick it, and they called a truce to bury the dead. They buried them all – French, Irish, British, and yeomen in an old fort right near where Thomas Gibbons lived. When they were making the new road into Aghagower some years ago, they came on some of the soldiers' graves and bones.

Johnny Gibbons, a relative of Tommy Gibbons, had gone to Ballinamuck with over one thousand men from around the Castlebar area, and he suffered his fate there.

Once the truce was called that ended the fighting, and it was not resumed after the burying of the dead. Denis Browne was called over to London to answer for his cowardly behaviour in the fight. Before he left, he appointed the strongest and best of his yeoman from among the tenants to guard Mount Browne 'til he'd come back. He had ten or twelve of them. They were obliged to do so as that was the system in those days. Then he left. However, the yeomen were not able to guard and protect the house properly when it was attacked by the local people.

The first thing taken was Browne's feather bed that he used to play pitch and toss in with his women. They hauled it out the door with ropes. There must have been room in the bed for nine or ten people. It was still kept in the parish of Aghagower to this day in the village of Meneen, off the Ballinrobe road.

Another fellow took a clock which was a rare thing then, and he hoisted it up on his back, and when the clock got shaken, it began to ring, and he flung it down and ran away. Some other lads picked it up and carried it off.

When it was all over, they didn't leave a flaming thing inside the walls of the house. The wine and brandy in the cellar were all gone.

The greater part of the house contents were taken away in the dead of the night and hidden in places all over the area. The bully man that was in charge let the local people rattle on at it.

One morning me grandfather was going to Sunday Mass, and he saw two men going out on a shaking mire wetland, and he wondered what they'd be doing there. After breakfast himself and some of the boys went out to investigate. They followed the trail and what did they find but a keg of brandy buried in the bog. They took it home, and he invited all the boys and girls from the whole neighbourhood for that night. They danced until clear daylight in the morning, and all went home blind drunk. Some of the men had hid some of the Browne's dishes and delph ware out in the nearby bogs, but they sank in to the bog and were never seen again.

When Denis Browne came back from London, he saw the awful state of his house with windows broken and all the contents gone. He sent out the yeomen to capture every damn one of the thieves. In time, he had them all arrested and taken as prisoners.

He sentenced the greater part of them to be transported, and he hung three or four of them. Browne said, 'Whatever else the rest of ye are going to get, you'll get the gallows anyway.' From that time on Denis was called 'Gallows Browne'. People knew enough after that never to mention that name to them, as the family would be most annoyed.[11]

꧁

Rory of the Hill: A Poem

Ye banished sons of Erin who with sighing went away,
Those gallant men with pikes and guns will come
      another day.
The blackheads and the kyloes, their homes and valleys
      are filled,
And from Tallybaun we'll rout them all, says Rory of the
      Hill.
I'm the bold Kilgeever mountaineer, and I'm Rory of the
      Hill.
I know I won't be welcome to Uggool or Dadreen,
Where nothing but the canny Scotch and sheepdog can
      be seen.
If their torrential ferns are not smashed by Gladstone's Bill,
To hell with Billy and his billy, says Rory of the Hill.[12]

꧁

Eviction of Ellen Coyne Jordan

Me mother's name was Ellen Coyne, and she married me father from Inishnakillew, but me father died young. She owed a year and a half's rent on the land in Inishnakillew to James McDonnell, the magistrate in Westport, who was also a sub-sheriff at that time. He had processed her for non-payment of the year and half's rent. In his sheriff's capacity, he came out to the island and put the lock on the door.

A friend of McDonnell had approached him expressing an interest in the land in Inishnakillew, and he offered to be a co-partner in the holding with McDonnell. One day the two of them came out to the house. While standing inside the door, his friend says to McDonnell, 'Will you give me the grass on this land, sir?'

'Yes,' says McDonnell. 'You can have the grass, potatoes, and oats.'

There was nothing left for me widowed mother to do. There was a dozen police there with McDonnell. All the furniture, the dresser, table, beds, and all were taken and placed outside the door, so that everything was outside the door. The sub-sheriff locked the door and that was it.

Then, me mother went out to her sister's house, out to James Máille's in Roscahill – with five orphans, three boys and two girls, and the youngest was about two. She wanted to get her land back. She got hold of a book and went round to her neighbours begging for enough money to pay the rent. After some time, she managed to get enough to pay the rent, for the neighbours were sympathetic and didn't want her and her orphans to be homeless. There was no land agitation in those days. When she had got the rent, she went in to McDonnell's office in Westport and insisted that he take the money. He wouldn't take the rent because he was in favour of giving the holding to his friend.

One day a little later McDonnell sent Willie Browne, who was an agent acting for his father, Paddy Browne of Drumgarue, out near Rosmoney in Kilmeena, to see if there was anything happening to the crops – the grass, potatoes and oats – and if so to advise him of their status. By this time, me mother was in rags when Willie was coming. She heard that Willie was going to Inishnakillew, and so she went along with him. He asked her to point out any place where any potatoes had been dug since she was evicted or dispossessed. She went all round the place and wasn't there a pit of potatoes dug that wasn't dug when she was evicted.

She says to Willie, 'Willie, this pit of potatoes wasn't dug when I left here.'

McDonnell's friend who wanted to get the holding and was expecting it, said to Willie that me mother had dug them up before. She got into an argument then with him saying they weren't dug up at that time. The man started to get flustered and frustrated and ending up making a clout at her. She summonsed him for assault in the courts. This was the only way she could get her case heard in the courts – outside of the landlord system. She had actually received this advice got from Willie Browne himself as he had told her that this was the only way to bring the entire matter before the regular courts and away from just the landlord.

Jimmy McDonnell was actually the magistrate in the court, but when he went to the court for the hearing, he decided not to sit on the bench that day and let Lord Browne of Westport decide the case. In a week after that James McDonnell had that bailiff send for her to settle with her. She went up to Westport to his office. The agent told her not to settle-up with him 'til he'd divide the land into two parts and settle on the rent for each. Now it had to be made into two even parts and allotted by a survey. McDonnell promised her he would divide the land. Soon after, he sent down a man by the name of George Walsh, who was a surveyor, and divided the land evenly and allotted the parts accordingly. There was no more trouble about that holding ever again.

One day me mother was going in to town, and McDonnell happened to be walking out of his house and met me mother on the road.

'Well, Mrs Jordan,' says he, 'how are you going on now with your co-partner?'

'Oh, he's alright, Mr McDonnell,' says she.

'What's wrong with you?' says he. 'You're not looking good.'

'Well, your honour, every time I see you, I tremble as I'm that much afraid of you.'

'Don't be afraid of me, Mrs Jordan,' says he, 'I'll be your best friend.'

McDonnell didn't live long after that, only a year or so, and he had indeed been a friend to her.[13]

Why Denis Browne Ceased His Hangings

Denis Browne, known as Gallows Browne or Browne the Bad, treated many of the people who broke in to his house in his own way, and shortly after, he took sick and died.

Later there was another Denis Browne, and he was as good as

he was bad and as ugly looking a man as anyone could ever see. He used to bother the neighbours, but in the end, he didn't live very long. Denis Browne never married but he was as good as his father for leaving bastards all around, hands down.

Now John Browne, Denis the Bad's son, came in and was a real gent.

There was an old ash tree on the lawn there near the house, and it was known as the 'hanging tree' as it was used by the Brownes for hangings.

Denis Browne's own nephew, who was an officer in the local British militia, stopped his uncle from hanging priests or anyone else for ever more, and this is how that happened. One day the militia soldiers were drilling on the lawn at Mount Browne, and the nephew was a young officer in the yeomen militia and was present that day. Just at that time Seán an tSagairt had rounded up a young priest and brought him up to Denis Browne to get a death sentence passed on him. If a priest were found in the community, it usually meant that he would receive the death penalty. The priest was brought before Denis Browne because he was a magistrate and could then decide whether to pass the death sentence on him.

Just then, the young officer rushes up to Browne, and says, 'Uncle Denis, what are you doing there?'

Browne replies, 'I'm signing this priest's death warrant, as he was caught and he knows the penalty.' The young priest was there beside him.

'Let that priest go,' says the young officer.

'No, I won't,' says Browne. 'He's going to be hanged right away.'

'Sign his release on the spot, Uncle Denis,' he says, 'or I promise you, you'll be in eternity before the priest.' He took out his revolvers and left one on the table and held the other in his hand. 'Take that revolver, Uncle,' says he, 'if you want to hang the priest.'

'If that's the way it is,' says Denis, 'we'll have to do what you say.' So, he signed the priest's release.

The nephew takes the release, hands it to the priest, and says, 'You take this and be going.' He was overcome with thanks.

'While you're at it, Uncle Denis,' says the nephew quickly, 'there's another little job that you should do. Sign this document here that you'll never hang another priest,' he says, 'nor no other man no more than a priest.'

Denis was astounded at his nephew's behaviour, but he signed the document anyway.

'Hand me that now,' says his nephew to him when he had it signed.

The nephew picked up the signed document and walked out to his superior officer, delivered the document to him, threw off his red coat and threw down his two revolvers. 'I'm after doing this,' he says, 'and you can do what you wish with me now.'

The officer in charge clapped him on the back. 'Good boy,' he says, 'if we had more of your sort, we wouldn't have half the murders that there are in Ireland.' He promoted him for his bravery.[14]

Denis Browne Had Bingham Do His Hanging

One day there was a young man walking across the Mount Browne farm, and Denis Browne saw him and went over to talk to him gently.

'What are you doing here?' says Denis.

'Oh, doing nothing much, sir, just walking,' says the young man. Denis immediately took out some paper and wrote out a note and asks him, 'Could you bring this letter to Mr Bingham in Castlebar?'

Perhaps Denis thought the young man had seen him doing something that Denis didn't want to have anyone outside know about. Anyway, the man accepted the note and continued on his way.

Now, the young man was a lazy kind of a man and didn't want to be bothered to go to Castlebar, but he met a man who said he was going to Castlebar. He asked that man if he would take and deliver Denis' letter to Mr Bingham so that he wouldn't have to bother. Perhaps he thought that it might be an honour for the other man to meet Mr Bingham or that he might get some reward. The other man took the letter and delivered it to Mr Bingham, and Mr Bingham hanged him immediately when he read it for it was written, 'Hang the Bearer.'[15]

Lucan Ploughs the Hearth Stones of Aghadrinagh

Lord Lucan tried to get elected to Parliament in 1857. He had been in the Crimean War in 1854 and caused the slaughter of the Light Brigade. Ousley Higgins of James Street, Westport, beat him in the election, and some of the election officers told Lucan when the election was over that he only got three votes in the little village of Aghadrinagh, near Castlebar on the Ballinrobe road. Now there was forty-seven houses in that village, and at that time only the man who was the head of the house had a vote. When Lucan heard of his low tally in that village, he said he'd plough under the hearth stones of Aghadrinagh, and he kept his promise not too long before 1859.

It was on the 1st of November that Lucan's men gave notice of eviction to the people with holdings in the village around Aghadrinagh, just as it was starting to get cold. Given what was going on generally in the area and because of the election results, the people were expecting that their eviction would eventually come. After that terrible day until the day he died, one of the tenants from there spoke of Lucan saying, 'Bad luck to his bones in the ground.' After his eviction, he moved to Glaspatrick.

In Aghadrinagh, the houses weren't levelled if you had the furniture out of the house, it was yours to keep and carry off, but if you hadn't the furniture out, then they'd put three crowbars together in it and they'd pull down the side of the house on top of the furniture, and so the family lost everything.

The house my grandfather, Pat O'Malley, lived in was the last house they knocked down because it was late in the evening. They left one room standing. When the brigade came down to the road and their work done, Pat O'Donnell of Castlebar, a bailiff for Lucan, stood on top of a little height there, and he saw the one small room left standing. He immediately sent the brigade back up again, and they finished the day's work completely with not one house standing. The people were expecting them to come.

When Lucan's brigade came to evicting some of the Mortimers from the village of Carrowmacloughlin, near Glaspatrick, they handled the eviction rather delicately because there had been incidents there when those Mortimers had been evicted by Lord Sligo.[16]

⌇

Evictions

After the Famine, there were many evictions all over the place. One of the worst landlords in the area was Lord Lucan. He lived in Castlebar and owned many estates including lands in Kilmeena, Glaspatrick, Arderry in Aghagower, and Oughty in Drummin. Lucan was especially attentive to clearing tenants off their holdings if they could not pay their rent. Moving people away became a standard process involving knocking the houses down.

In Glaspatrick on the 6th of April 1859, Lucan's crowbar brigade invaded the village. They pulled down one hundred houses that day, and they left one hundred families sleeping under the open air that night. Not too far away in the big house in Murrisk, Marina Lodge, a sister of Lord Lucan lived and was married to a man by the name of Lindsay. They had a big party there that night at the Lodge, while five hundred people were sleeping nearby in the open under the sky.[17]

⌇

Sir Neal O'Donel of Newport Helps Kilmeena Men

Throughout Ireland in the year of the Great Famine of Black 1847, people were starving, and there were people out in Kilmeena who were also starving. Some of the men in Kilmeena were agitating against their landlord, Sir Neal O'Donel of Newport House. They were agitating to get relief for something to eat and Sir Neal was not sympathetic.

Sir Neal had arranged to meet with some of the people at the bridge of Buckfield. The men wanted to show their determination hoping that they would get relief from their landlord as they were starving. Sir Neal had organised the local militia of yeomen and the king's army intending to subdue the people by cutting them down and thus not having to put up with any shouting or demonstration by them. He sent word to the Kilmeena people to meet him at the Buckfield Bridge and pronounced that if any of them crossed the bridge, they would die. Now the people had gathered in a big gang on one side of the bridge. After talking together, they decided that it was as well for them to die fighting as to die starving of hunger.

The first two of them linked their arms and started to march across the bridge. Then Sir Neal saw the next two men also link arms and start to march across the bridge. Even though Sir Neal was commander of the militia and the British army soldiers, he appreciated his difficulty and said, 'It's no use killing them because they're willing to die.' So, he sent them all home, and in a fortnight's time, he organised famine relief to come to their assistance. Sir Neal by settling the claim of the first two men coming across the bridge, he was able to make a claim for the relief assistance.[18]

⌘

The Dead Along the Glenkeen Road

During the second year of the Famine in 1847 the relief office in Westport were ordered to deliver meal and to land the relief shipment in Carrowmore. As a result of the interference by Mick Carroll, who was a relief agent in Louisburgh, he managed to have the orders changed to have the relief landed up at Bundarragha instead. He had the ship come in to the Killaries, and then the meal had to be carried over a poor road to Bundarragha. He made that change so that the job would last longer, for if the meal had landed into Carrowmore, the work wouldn't last long at all or maybe he thought he might be mobbed by the crowd there.

At that time anyone entitled to get relief was able to get four stones of Indian meal. Now, they made arrangements to have sheds available in Bundarragha to store the relief meal since the boat house where they landed was all filled. All those who lived in Glenkeen and needed to get relief had to go on the ould course path from Glenkeen to Bundarragha. Many people made that trek to get the meal, but half of them died on the roadside before they landed back home with their half hundred weight of meal.

There was a woman by the name of Mrs Scanlon who lives back behind in Six Noggins, and they were in desperate need of relief. Didn't she and her poor husband set off to get their share of the relief. On their return trip from Bundarragha carrying their heavy relief bags, didn't he collapse on her when they were near Doolough. She stuck him on her back along with the half hundred weight of meal and walked on. After a while she landed him in to the only house she could see in Glencullin, and that was still the only house there to this day. She left the husband there, and she had three miles of a wild rugged mountain path on Mweelrea Ben to travel to her home with the meal. She left the meal at home and travelled back 'til she landed abroad in Glencullin again and stuck her husband on her back again 'til she landed him at home.

Herself and himself lived there in Glenkeen 'til they were evicted in 1852. They were hurled out of their lands and farm there by the landlord, Lord Lucan. After that, the two of them packed up, left their old home, and landed abroad in England. Ten or twelve years later they landed back in the lowland of Furgill and lived there until he died on her. After that the poor widow woman was going around spinning and carding wool in the parish and calling on relations and neighbours to do pieces of work in their houses. She eventually became too weak to work, and she died in the poor house. But before the time she died, she had been able to save some money, and she left it to her relations.

Carroll died in Louisburgh, and he hadn't any luck.

In those Famine days when some of the dead were examined, they found nothing in their stomachs but a bit of raw Indian meal.[19]

The Jumper

One time there was a man from Dooghmakeon, and he felt so hard pressed from the Famine days that he decided to become a jumper, and so he became a Protestant in the way some people did at that time. After that, life for him in the village of Dooghmakeon became too hot and difficult for him as he was ignored by all his neighbours and friends. He couldn't lead a normal life in terms of buying and selling as he needed. Finally, he couldn't stand the isolation and decided to depart. He settled down somewhere east of Castlebar, not too far from Bohola, and got married to a Protestant woman.

Years later his brother who still lived in Dooghmakeon and a neighbour of his were going to the well in Loughkeeraun near Bohola to make a station for the health of the horses and the cattle during the year. It was thought that the jumper brother lived quite close to this Loughkeeraun well. The brother's wife told her husband to call in to his brother's house and to find how he was doing since he left Dooghmakeon.

At the end of three days the two men returned from Loughkeeraun and were loud in their praises of the jumper brother and his wife. They had the best of eating and drinking when they visited them. The neighbouring man agreed entirely and said the only difficulty had been that she had said something one time.

'What did she say?' says the brother's woman, her curiosity being all stirred up.

'It's doesn't really matter now what she said,' says her husband, but the woman persisted until at last the husband told what she had said.

'She said that the Catholic religion wasn't much.'

'I hope,' says the wife, 'you made her a good answer, the hussy.'

'I made no answer at all,' says the husband.

'And why didn't you answer her?' says the wife.

'Because she was filling my plate for the third time with beef, and it wasn't the time nor the place to answer her back,' says the husband.[20]

⁓

A Girl Is Taken from the Bird's Nest

Grady of Cloonlaur in Killeen married Mary McHale, a cousin of Grady's brother-in-law. He and his wife had a child, Maggie. They were so hard pressed for food during the Famine times that they talked about making plans for Maggie. They made arrangements in case they might die of starvation to give Maggie to the Bird's Nest, a colony in Achill. They lived on a while after that but for not too long and then died. Maggie was a fine handsome young girl, and she was sent to the Bird's Nest as was arranged.

Now, Tony McHale, Mary's brother, was a small man, as was Mary, and was also living in Cloonlaur. After Mary's death, Tony and some other family members went all the way over to Achill to Dugort to take Maggie out of the Bird's Nest colony. Tony had a plan, and he went to a Catholic house just near the colony and had someone from that house send in a messenger to Maggie asking her to come out to get a message. When Maggie came out, Tony and his friends quickly seized her and took her off with them. Immediately, they were followed by a drove of other jumpers who came out after Maggie to take her back to the colony. Tony fought them with his stick and some other Catholic neighbours helped defend Maggie and fended off the drove. Tony brought the child to the convent in Westport and later she went over to America.

As it happened, Tony had a holding of land in the lands near another colony located at Clapperbridge over the Bunleemslough River in Bunlahinch near Killeen. In spite for what Tony had done in taking Maggie away from the Achill colony, a man by the name of Rorey gave a sworn statement to Lord Sligo that Tony's holding was from a certain man and that that man had actually died and that therefore Tony would have to forfeit the holding. Lord Sligo took a legal action against Tony based on the informer's evidence because he wanted to let the land to another jumper. In the end Tony was thrown out of his land. However, a neighbour out of kindness gave Tony a conacre of bad land. He was still able to sow there in late April, and he'd always have the best crop in the area.[21]

⌘

Billy Madden, Process Server, Runs in His Pelt

Billy Madden was a process server for the Westport district which included Clare Island. He was a good friend of James McDonnell, who was a local magistrate in Westport. Madden used Patrick Ruddy as a sub-process server to make actual delivery of the processes, and he has used him for serving on Clare. Now, Madden had a big job to do servicing processes to all the residents of Clare, every single soul there.

One evening Madden went out to this Ruddy man in Louisburgh that was supplying provisions in to Clare, and he never got much money for his service. Madden asked him if the night was fit for him to go in to Clare. The man said it was. Madden gave Ruddy a bag of processes and the fare to Clare and told him to deliver the bag of processes to Clare and to deliver a process to every soul in Clare the following day. Well, Ruddy went home and prepared himself to go to Clare.

The following day, Ruddy came out and hired a boat and went in to Clare. He had many first and second cousins all over Clare, and so was familiar with the place. He had his bag of processes with him. Now, there wasn't a single woman or man or child in Clare that wasn't down on the green by the castle with sticks and stones and all as his boat was approaching. Ruddy and his boat wouldn't be let within a mile of the quay, and so he had to turn round and go back home and inform Billy Madden in Westport.

Now, the next day Madden himself went out to Roonah with his bag of processes and took the mail boat, which was run by Grady, who acted like a sub-bailiff belonging to the McDonnell. Grady had been given the running of the post boat, but he did other work as well. Madden asked him to land the boat at the far western end of the island, near Toormore, so that he'd commence serving the processes over there and walk his way to the quay.

There was a poor woman down that western end of the island, Mrs Billy Gibbons, an O'Malley of the Halloran Máilles, and she was coming up from the shore there with some four or five girls after cutting lichen which they used for dyeing. Her husband was abroad in Colorado at the time. Just as Madden was on the brink of a rise coming from Toormore at the far end of the island, she says, 'Girls, now's our time.' She went back then towards Toormore where Madden was coming up from, and with the girls, she took hold of him and took the bag off him. She put the bag in the bottom of the cave, the deepest cave in Clare, and it was never seen since. Then, they took every stitch of clothing off Billy Madden and let him go bare naked over past the church all the way to the green by the quay. Madden had to get some clothes from Grady and went out home to Westport without ever serving a single process that day.[22]

⤳

How Billy Madden Ate His Processes

Billy Madden was a process server. He lived in Westport and was sent in to Clare Island to serve the processes on all the people there. Austin Grady, who ran the post boat, would bring him in from Roonah, and he often brought in police with him for protection. Madden was a half landlord himself.

Now, this day that Madden came to serve the processes, the women gathered. Mary Máille, a Gibbons woman, Mrs Mickey Gibbons, was in charge of the women. They brought Madden with them back to a gap in the cliff, took the processes off him, gave him a good mauling, and took the clothes of him. When they took his bag of processes, they said to him:

'Take out your processes for you're trying to make beggars of us and our children and try them on yourself. Now go ahead and eat them.'

They made him eat them all, one by one, before they let him go.

Madden had to return to Westport without accomplishing his mission. After that they arranged to process the islanders by posting copies of the original process on the courthouse door in Louisburgh, often forty at a time, and a copy was given to the court. The courthouse was opposite the police barracks. The tenants would be decreed from that then. Pat Ruddy, the sub-process server, would prove service in the court unless the lawyer admitted service.

There was often seen the long carts of police going in to Roonah with helmets and rifles so as to seize the cattle on the island, but they'd come back empty. The cattle on the island would all be driven in to the O'Malleys' farm in Ballytoohy for they'd have paid their rent, and the cattle couldn't be seized.[23]

⁓

The Marked Ring the Officer Would Not Cross

In 1882 a rule was passed by the court in Westport that a landlord or his agent could legally serve a process on a tenant by placing a copy of the process on the door of the courthouse or local barracks and sending the original process by registered letter.

The landlord of Clare Island wanted to ensure that the process was properly carried out, and so he arranged for gun boats, police and officers to assemble, and they all landed within in Clare. The senior officer came on the shore at the quay, and he had one hundred police with him, but they stayed on the boat outside. The priest came down to meet the officer on the road opposite Flynns and O'Gradys. The priest drew a round circle on the road, and he told the officer that if he crossed that circle, he'd be sorry for it. The officer was stunned and gave the matter some thought. Then he returned to his boat and took off out of there.

Within a short period, the Congested Districts Board had the island bought, and it was the third large estate to be bought in Ireland under the Purchase of Land Act of 1891 which established the CDB.

Later the islanders composed a little song to commemorate Billy Madden:

He went to the end of the island, to a village called Toormore,

And instead of being saluted, they had stones for him in store.

Madden ran like a hare before the hound,

And never looked behind him 'til he reached Billy's Pound.[24]

ॐ

How Tom McDonnell Settled with His Clare Tenants

Tom McDonnell of Clonna was a terrible gentleman. He had bought Clare Island from Lord Lucan for a little estate for himself. He sent in an accountant to demand rent from his tenants, and he couldn't collect any rent. The next thing he did was to bring in mounted soldiers and police in a steamer 'til he landed within in

Clare. Didn't the parish priest there, Father Murphy, who was an awful strong man, take on McDonnell.

'Well, Murphy,' says he to the priest, 'I've bought this island, and indeed, it was dear enough.'

The island tenants demanded that he reduce the rent by four shillings in the pound, and Fr Murphy supported them.

'Well, McDonnell,' says the priest, 'you'll not turn one soul of them outside the door of their houses today. Go and give the tenants four shillings and settle the pound reduction.'

'I'll not do that, Murphy.'

'I'll make you do it, McDonnell,' says the priest. Now McDonnell was a magistrate as well as the landlord, and he would have the law on his side.

'I cannot,' says he, 'having bought the island so dear.'

'Be leaving this island now,' Fr Murphy says to him, 'and this's a spot you'll never leave yer foot on again.'

McDonnell backed down without saying anything more and left Clare the way he came with all the soldiers and police. In a week's time, hadn't he an account sent in to each of the islanders that he was going to give them the four shillings reduction in the pound. In a few weeks after that, he took to his bed, and he never left it 'til he went to the grave. His daughters then were collecting the rent for a few years afterwards, but they decided to sell the island to the Congested Districts Board. That put an end to the landlords in Clare, and the land was eventually returned to the people.[25]

Sir Samuel O'Malley's Estate Lands

When Sir Samuel O'Malley's children had grown up, he left the family home at Rose Hill and settled by himself in Kilboyne, near Castlebar where he also had lands. He had spent considerable sums of money earlier and was deep in debt. He decided to mortgage his lands and estate to the Law Life Insurance Company in order to borrow money to pay down some of his debts. Later on, the Law Life Insurance started systematically evicting tenants from his lands, as was common and practical for them in those famine years. This landlord had made up a rule that if a tenant wasn't able to pay two years' rent in advance, the tenant and his family would be evicted, and their house knocked down.

Every family in this island of Inishnakillew was to be turned out if they couldn't pay two years' rent. John Quinn's house, just below here, had two crowbars stuck under the four rafters by the crowbar brigade. He had a wife, a woman by the name of Mary Walsh, who was desperate to save her house and furniture. The man who was the master of the crowbar brigade, knocking the houses down for the Law Life Insurance, was a man by the name of Captain Walsh.

Says she to him, 'I thought one of me own name i'd never knock down the house down over me.'

Capt. Walsh says to her, 'Is your name Walsh?'

'Well,' says she, 'it is.'

And so, he called on the crowbar brigade to put up their crowbars and go on to the next house. At least Capt. Walsh had a heart in him.

Me grandmother lived in that house behind them with five orphans and her husband dead, but luckily, she was able to pay the two years' rent. All the men and their families had to leave Inishnakillew, but me grandmother, Marie Máille, Máire Hughey, stuck it out, and I'm now the last of the Jordans in the island. I am the last of the Jordans living on the island.[26]

❧

The Last of the O'Malleys

Now, once upon a time, the Danes ruled in this part of Ireland, and they didn't like the O'Malleys. They had done battle together many a time over their long-lasting feud, and finally the Danes won out. They passed a law that all men with the O'Malley name would be killed. The O'Malley men were all rounded up and hung or had their heads cut off.

At the time there was this O'Flaherty woman, and she married an O'Malley. They lived out in Connemara with her father, as he had married in to that O'Flaherty house. Her father was stone-blind. When the Danes found out that there was an O'Malley man living there, he was taken off and killed. It turned out then that the woman was going to have a youngster, and so the Danes put a guard on her house until her child was born. When they discovered the child was a female, they took the guard off the house saying, 'We have no business here anymore.'

One night the mother of the young girl had a dream that if she brought her child to St Brendan's Well in Kilmeena on Good Friday before the sun would rise and put the child down in to the well three times, the child would come up the third time as a boy. The mother had this dream three nights in a row, one after the other. She told her father about her dream, and he said, 'In the name of God, a stór, nothing ever beats a trying.'

The young mother made secret preparations to go visit Brendan's Well early on Good Friday morning, and she put the young girl down in the well, and on dipping her for the third time, the child came up as a little boy. The mother who was then living in Moyna in Kilmeena realised the danger she and her boy were in if the Danes found out that her little child was now a male O'Malley child. She knew that the child would be beheaded. So, she started to make plans to save him. At that time lugger boats or hookers used to come in to Moyna and from there would go to Scotland. She made plans to get away from Kilmeena with her boy and went to Scotland. She settled somewhere outside of where Glasgow would later be. Eventually she got married to a man with the name Bailey, and with the Bailey man, she had two sons.

The three little boys all grew up together and were the best of friends. They were good and hardy fellows, and they played well together all sorts of games. One game was called 'kicking a cod' and consisted of kicking a piece of old cloth packed with hay. The Máille boy was a little bit older and usually he used to outkick the two Bailey boys or indeed win at most any other game they would play, and sometimes he would even knock them down. One day the boys were kicking the cod, and they were having a bit of rough play. The Máille boy hurt one of the Bailey boys for he says to him, 'You bloody bastard, what's your name?' The Máille boy got vexed at being called a bastard, left them playing and walked in to his mother.

'Mother,' says he, 'am I a bastard?'

'You are not, son,' says she, 'and why do you ask?'

'Before I leave here,' says he, 'you'll have to tell how and what I am or I'll take your life.'

Then, she had to sit him down and tell him everything that went on with his O'Malley people, and how his father and all the other O'Malley men were killed.

'Well,' says he, 'since the Danes killed all my people, they'll have to kill me or I'll kill them.'

The O'Malley boy decided that he would go back to Ireland and bring vengeance on the Danes. When the two Bailey boys heard the story and saw how he was making plans to return to Ireland, they said that wherever he would go, they would go along with him.

The three of them then got prepared to return to Ireland, and they went back by boat 'til they came along to Westport Quay. From there they headed out to Connemara where the blind grandfather lived. When they arrived at the house the two younger Bailey boys went in to talk to the grandfather saying that they were O'Malleys. He asked the older Bailey boy to put out his hand, and he did.

'There's not a drop of O'Malley blood in your body,' says the old blind man.

Then, the younger Bailey did the same and put forth his hand. Again, the old man says, 'There's not a drop of O'Malley in your body either.'

When the third fellow came up and says the same as the other two, the old man says, 'You're the real O'Malley, indeed,' and he was overjoyed to greet his grandson.

Then the three young men chatted with the old man about the history of the O'Malleys. After that, the O'Malley man went around amongst his O'Malley relations and talked to them about what the Danes had done and how they could have their revenge and do away with them.

At that time the mails were run from Dublin all the way to Roonah Quay. The soldier running the mail rode on a white horse and was dressed in a white suit of clothes too. The way the bridle path was going was away back along the shore, and over the years the riding over the bridle path had worn down the side of the hill so that the path was well below the level of the land on either side. The O'Malley man stood behind a whitethorn bush and knocked the soldier off his saddle as he rode by. He pulled his sword out of his scabbard and cut off his head with his first wallop. Then he took off the soldier's uniform and put it on himself, and he took the soldier's white horse and rode on to Roonah on the very path that the postman used to go.

When the postman from Clare Island came in to Roonah, the O'Malley lad hid himself behind a skelp of rock. When the postman landed, the O'Malley cut the head off him. Now, he had killed two of them. When the O'Malley's friends saw what he had done and the way he done it, they thought a lot of him, held him in high regard, and they all rallied to him. When the two Bailey boys saw what their brother had done, they changed their names from Bailey over to O'Malley. He mobilised all his relations and friends together and many others came out to help him. Soon after that they backed the Danes entirely out of this part of the country. The three brothers all settled down in the West and from them the O'Malley family is supposed to have descended.[27]

History of the Ó Máilles in the West

Once the Ó Máilles were made extinct by the Lavelles, who had one eye in their forehead, and whatever the eye would envy, it would burn and melt. They were a fierce lot, and they wanted to kill all the Ó Máilles in those parts.

Finally, there was only one boy of the Ó Máilles left. His mother had remarried after her Ó Máille husband had been killed by the Lavelles. Then, she had two other boys. The three young men were bent on having their revenge on the Lavelles. They came out from Prospect near Killadangan in Louisburgh where there was a man of the name of Heraty, and he was blind. He had his sight once but lost it. The young men walked up to him and said that they were three Ó Máilles. He said he'd tell them if they were.

'Give me your hand,' says Heraty, 'and I'll know whether you are or not.'

The youngest man put out his hand, and the old man said, 'There's not a drop of Ó Máille in ye, and ye can be going off.'

The second man heard the same thing.

The third young man came in and put out his hand.

'You're an Ó Máille,' says the old man, 'wherever you come from, and now,' says he, 'are ye going to have yer revenge on the Lavelles?'

The old man told them that there was one of the Lavelles in a hole in Derryheeagh near Cregganbaun. The three of them laid siege to that Lavelle place, and suddenly the Lavelle took off on his heels running as fast as he could down to the little islands in the bay where there was another Lavelle living. The Ó Máilles caught up to him when he was stepping in to the boat, and they let his head fall on the seat of the boat, and he was killed. Conn Uisce Lavelle was his name after that.

Then to disguise himself the Ó Máille put on the Lavelle's outer garment, and he killed the other Lavelle on that island. Then, all three headed for Furmoyle, and they gave chase to the Lavelle that was living there 'til he went down to where Carrownisky school was, and they killed that man there.[28]

Teacher of Navigation

There was an old schoolmaster here in Inishnakillew, and they used to call him Feeney. He'd stay a month in one house and then a month in another house. The children were going to school in the island at that time, and they'd be even grown boys and girls. Feeney could even teach navigation up to the standard that would take a man around the world. Feeney would have his school in one house, and all the other students would come there from Inishnakillew and Inishcottle. He was a homeless man himself, a traveller. I don't know where he belonged to, but he could do great things. He didn't finish his life in here on this island.

Once a young lad came in to see Feeney at the school, and Feeney asks him, 'What do you want to learn?'

'I want to learn navigation,' says the lad.

'But you need to learn mensuration before you come to navigation,' says Feeney.

I think he was a boy by the name of Hill, that's what I heard the old people saying. Feeney learned him mensuration, but Hill didn't stick with it.

There were very good students in Inishnakillew a hundred and thirty years ago. The islanders then would only bring in the best teachers to teach their children. They had to pay their teachers just as everyone else. Some of the islanders put up the teachers in their house, and one didn't put one up without learning a great deal from him.

I seen a lot of people living here in Inishnakillew that went on the Free Immigration Plan to America. A man by the name of Jamsie Kearns went out from Inishcottle for America, and his son is now a big lawyer in Chicago. I think he was Mayor of Chicago for a while. He was only ten years old when he went. I seen the ship he went out on; she came in well to the south side of Clare Island, near Old Head. It was a steamboat, a big white ship. I was back on the beaches at Inishoo, and I saw her. The passengers were taken out to the ship from Westport Quay in tenders. For that immigration plan, you had to sign your name up to join the Union Army.

I think the landlords of Ireland had a lot to do with clearing people away from the country by evicting them. Me mother, who was then widowed, was in favour of going and bringing the family with her. We were small then, of course. Her brother wanted her to take out the whole family. She'd met a man by the name of Dever, Pat Dever, and he came from where her brother was living in America.

'Now, Pat,' says she, 'I have encouragements from me brother to go out on the free immigration.'

'Your brother,' says he, 'can give you a free house, and there's no mistake about that, but how will you keep your family together? You'll go and work to rear them yourself. Then, the first one that grows up when he's ready, he'll walk out of the house to take care of himself and gets married and leaves you then or maybe even before that. Then, the next one will do the same. And then when you want them, you won't know where they are. Now, if you stay at home here, whatever little hardships you may have, you'll be with your children and your family 'til they're fit to look out for themselves in their full strength.'

She took Pat's advice. She didn't leave, and she never was sorry. Her family stayed with her until she put them everywhere to get a living. There's two of them out now in America, the ouldest and the youngest.[29]

Teacher Walks On Water

There was a teacher by the name of Feeney who used to teach on this island of Inishnakillew from time to time. He taught in the village school along with another teacher, and their scholars would come in to them there from the other islands.

One day the scholars began to humbug Feeney, and they annoyed him.

'You're in an island now, master, and you'll have to stay in it 'til the tide goes out for now for nobody will leave you out by boat.'

Feeney went straight out of the school over to Kelly's house and picked up a stick in his hand. It was high water at the time, and he tapped his stick on top of the water as he was going out and walked out on the water, tapping his stick on the top of the water as he was going out 'til he got out by this side of Claggan. The village people were all out watching him in amazement as he was able to find the stepping stones under the water even then. They had to see him do this feat.

There was about thirty-seven houses in Inishnakillew at that time. They kept a schoolteacher between the two islands, Inishnakillew and Inishcottle. It was said locally that Feeney was the best schoolteacher in Ireland.[30]

⌒

Captain Coney Saves Johnny Gibbons

Captain Coney of Aughris Beg, near Cleggan, was a captain in the South Mayo militia. He lived at Aughris in a commodious residence. He was a descendant of Planters, and thus had a good residence.

One day the outlaw, Johnny Gibbons, was out in his boat going about his usual business, and soon he found that he was being pursued by a Coast Guard cutter. Johnny was a good sailor, had a fine boat and knew his coastline well. He carefully navigated his boat so he would land a short distance away from Capt. Coney's residence. The local area was an open, wild, bleak district, and Johnny had no possible place in which to seek shelter. Now, he knew where Capt. Coney's house was, and he went up to it and asked to speak to Capt. Coney. The good captain was at home, and Gibbons asked him if he would place him under his protection.

The officers, who had been following Gibbons in their cutter, saw where he had landed and followed him onto the shore. They pursued him all the way to the captain's house. They were allowed in to see Capt. Coney, and they demanded to know where Gibbons was as they wanted to arrest him as an outlaw. Capt. Coney said that the outlaw would not be given up to them, that he was under his protection, and that they would not get him except across his own dead body. The officers were quite taken aback by the captain's position. They didn't insist on going any further, and they left the house.

Capt. Coney was a Protestant but kept the outlaw Gibbons safe for some days. His son became a Catholic.[31]

☙

The Fenian Who Used the Blood of the Goose

There were five men identified by an informer as being Fenians at the time of the Fenians, and they were told they would have to report in to the barracks in Castlebar to await their trial. Now, they knew that there were the races on that day at Breaghwy, near Castlebar. As they were walking in the leader of the group said he'd like to see the races if he could. Soon he saw a few geese beside the road, and he caught one of them and cut its head off and let its blood pour onto his own head and arms. When he got to the barracks, there was only one policeman there on account of the races. The leader reported that he had been badly beaten out on the road by a crowd of blaggards, and he wanted the policeman to go after them. The policeman said there was himself in the barracks, but he said he'd go on out and see what he could do about the blaggards. When the policeman had gone out, the leader went in to the guard room and got a revolver. Who did he meet there, but the informer Moran who was ranting on about death and life and tomorrow.

'Moran,' says the leader, 'make an Act of Contrition. You're going to die.' He shot him and then went to America. He was about eight or nine years in America, and this one evening, when he was going to have his supper, an American police detective landed in and had a shakehands with him and says, 'I'm looking for you this few weeks.'

'Well,' says the leader to the detective, 'sit down for a minute, and I'll bring you a pail of beer.' So, the leader went out of the bar and never came back.[32]

⬖

The Fenian Who Changed His Name

There was a Fenian brother, Pat McNicholas, from around Louisburgh who belonged to the organisation, and he had a pike and he hid the pike in the eave of the house. It appears that someone gave information to the police about him having a pike. The constables raided the house and after searching high and low, they found the pike. They arrested poor McNicholas and brought him to Louisburgh, where he was sentenced to be shot.

It appears McNicholas had some dealings with the minister in Westport, named Reverend Nicholson. He had sold the minister a mare or something, and they became acquainted. When the minister heard of the sentence, he went to work to try to get a reprieve. He got the reprieve and then as soon as he got it, he took his horse and galloped out from Westport to Louisburgh. McNicholas had been sentenced and was on his knees, and the shooting was ready to take place. The minister came in galloping up the street, and he was flaunting a paper in his hands. The military stood and looked, and as he jumped off his horse, he said, 'This man is reprieved.' The minister showed the reprieve to the man, and he got up and went on his way as his life had been spared.

The military were frustrated in not getting to shoot the man. They were hard out for blood, and they headed back to their station. As they went back up the street, they noticed a young man coming in over the bridge with a bag of oats to sell. Garvey was his name, and he was from Furmoyle near the bridge at Carrowniskey, up the mountain there. The military got a hold of Garvey, pulled him from his mare, and riddled him with bullets, shot him dead, when they were foiled from the other shooting.[33]

Fenians and Their Leaders in Westport Area

There were five hundred families in Kilmeena about forty years in the time of the land agitation, and the names of every man in the parish was known to the Fenian organisers. They were good in this parish. Fenianism was active in the parish of Kilmeena then, and indeed all over Ireland. The Fenians had a reputation, and they got credit for their actions. They included: Randall McDonell of Crow Hill, Westport, and Joe MacCanna were the leading men of them;

neither of them ever married. John Lavelle, John (Big John) Máille of Lower Bridge Street, Westport, and Pat Berry were also part of the ring leaders. The four of them would hold their meetings regularly in Westport.

The organisation included committee men in every village around, and a man in every railroad station.

Pat Quinn of Inishnakillew, John Quinn's father, who was a boatwright, and William Casey of Calen were the delegates representing the islands. The boys from all the islands would come together when there'd be drilling.

There were also the delegates from the Kilmeena parish who would go in to the little hall at the side of the chapel, and they'd meet there and sit round the table: Thomas Nolan and John Máille of Claggan, Pat Gibbons of Rosmindle (below Roscahill), Austin Gibbons of Carraholly (beside Rusheen), Edward Callanan of Cross, Pat Máille of Drumhuskert (by the Owenmaorockagh River), Thomas Gavin of Balyure, Willy Brown of Drumagh, Pat Kane of Gortawarla (by Rossow River), known as Long Michael Kane, and he was still hardy in 1940 at age seventy-eight, Pat Grady of Clooneen (below Drumhuskert) and William Fahey of Gobhathick in Derrinaraw.

When I was a young boy, I seen some of the arms meself. In this island there was a lot of them hidden in Pat Quinn's haggard. There was a rifle for every delegate in the parish; the common five-eighths had nothing. The men from Claggan and Roscahill brought their guns in to Inishnakillew. I seen them practice. One of them threw up a ball, and Pat Quinn fired at the ball, and it dropped straight out by the chapel in Moyna. He fired it on a calm day, and the splash was seen on the water. They were guns in a big wooden box on the ground, and there were two men ordering the others around on a fine summer day. That would have been after a parade when they had all assembled for drill the night before. The bullets were leaden, with a flat end and a round end, and were more than a half inch long.

In those days the police were afraid to go in to Inishnakillew at any time because it was such a difficult place to get in and out of in terms of the tide and the road. One time I remember the police came in around my family house and stayed all night. I felt their presence in the morning. When I went in to Kilmeena the next day, I says to one of the police, 'I smelt ye the other night, ye buggers. Ye were down in the islands.'

'Well, we smelt ye too,' says one of them. 'I nearly came in to the house for a bit of heat.'

'I'd give ye some heat,' says I, 'if ye did.'

Martin Mulchrone was active, and he was the father-in-law of Michael Kilroy of Newport, who was involved at the latter end of things.[34]

The Driving of Sligo's Cattle

In about 1900 the people from Aghagower on Sligo's estate had a meeting and decided to drive the cattle off Sligo's estate. There were two different Hibernian groups at the time, the American Alliance and the Board of Erin, and they both contributed to the effort. It was decided at the meeting that there should be a cattle drive.

This American man says, 'It's not the way to do it. There's enough of cattle driving going on through the county.'

Another fellow says, 'What would you do if there's enough of cattle driving?' 'I'll tell you what I'd do,' the American says, 'instead of driving the cattle away, I'd bring down the cattle to the estate office and give them up to the master.' The meeting listened to what the American had to say, and the whole group discussed his proposal. 'And how would you do it?' asks someone.

'Well, I'd send word to every man on the estate, whether he be his own cattle man or the landlord's man, Catholic or Protestant, as far as is convenient, and we'd order them all out and the man that doesn't come, we'll know what to do with him.'

There were many other suggestions, and all were discussed. Some said to make it like a national funeral. The conclusion was that all men should assemble, those with a horse and car, those with just a horse or an ass, or those who would just come on foot.

Word was sent round then to everybody within three or four miles all round. They all turned out in Aghagower. The young fellows went out on the Sligo estate gathering up the cattle on the big farms scattered over the mountain. The cattle were brought in by road from the farms and assembled in Aghagower. By the time the cattle were gathered up in Aghagower, there was a good procession of people there. 'Twas a very cold, wicked day, and the RIC sergeant was there standing in front of the cattle. Old John Knight told the sergeant what it was all about.

Knight says to me, 'I think there are a lot of lads inclined to fall back and I think it'll be left to you and me in the end to head the procession in to Westport. Are you game for it?'

'I am,' says I.

We headed the procession with the civic guard sergeant, and when the cattle would go to rush too fast, and we gave orders to take proper care of all the cattle. Behind the cattle were the mourning carriages, outside cars, traps, horses and saddles and men on foot. We all walked in to Westport from Aghagower. When we came to Westport station, we were halted by the old RIC from the barracks, about twenty-five of them, drawn up across the road. They had rifles and pointed pith helmets. They were ready to make a charge. John Knight went in ahead to the guard station and started to reason with them, and the other lads were trying to force the cattle through.

I reasoned with the fellows to keep quiet. I had a revolver, I suppose. There were plenty of them around. John Knight met and agreed with the RIC detective inspector. Lord Sligo's agent said there was nothing secret or violent about us and we were to give up the cattle to the Marquis of Sligo without any harm to them. Knight told the detective inspector to fall in behind the procession with his men behind us.

'Come on,' says Knight. 'Ye do your duty – we'll do ours.' The police fell in exactly as planned behind the cattle.

We marched down to Lord Sligo's agent's office, called for the agent, Bartlett Browne, and he came out. He sent down to the castle for men to come up to take charge of the cattle.

They came up with sticks and dogs and took away the cattle.

On a fair morning three days later, the RIC had rounded up some men, about twenty-five or thirty men, who had been part of the drive. There were two Manuses in the half parish included, Manus Kane, one of the leaders, and Manus Walsh who was a quiet inoffensive man.

Didn't they arrest Manie Walsh. When I heard of the arrests, I went in to the barracks for they didn't know my name.

'We didn't get your name,' says a policeman to me, 'but we know you know.'

'You can take me,' I says, 'if you like, but they didn't know or do anything.' All the men were released next day and returned for trial, but they got no sentence.

The Sligo farm in Aghagower was broken up by the Congested Districts Board as a result, and the tenants are back on their land again.

The tenants on the farm had been evicted in about 1860 by Sydney Smith, Sligo's agent.

He said to Sligo that the farm was the best land in Ireland for mountainy sheep or cattle. The result was that there was a notice to quit clapped on every man's door.[35]

✺

Why Cromwell Gave Cornfield to the Kellys

Cromwell was on his march way back in east Mayo and heading for the Midlands. He used always make it a habit to camp at night near water or on a river's bank. They were heading for the Shannon. As they were marching along there was an old soldier who couldn't keep up the pace of march. He was straggling and fell behind, and he knew for sure that he was going to be court-martialled when he arrived up late at the camp. He thought he'd have to make up some good story for Cromwell.

As the soldier was stumbling along, there was an old man, Kelly, who was digging spuds in the field on the side of the road. Kelly asks the soldier, 'Who was that at the head of the soldiers?'

'That's Cromwell,' says the soldier.

'I wish he was in Hell,' says Kelly.

When the soldier finally arrived up in the camp that evening, he was trying to think how he could save his own skin, so he told the story about Kelly. Cromwell sent some of his soldiers back for Kelly and told them to bring him, dead or alive. They brought Kelly back as a prisoner and thrust him before Cromwell.

'Well, my man,' says Cromwell, 'did you say you wished me to be in Hell?'

'I did, certainly,' says Kelly.

'And why did you say that?' asks Cromwell.

'I thought if you got in to Hell, you'd beat all the devils in Hell out of it.'

'Good for you, my man,' says Cromwell. 'Do you see that land as far as your eye can look all around you? That'll be yours and your heir's, as long as the grass grows or water runs.'

It's from that moment the famous Kelly of Cornfield sprang, the famous racing family. They kept fine horses and used to ride themselves.[36]

⁂

The Hospitality of Inishturk

There was once a chieftain in Meath by the name of O'Lorcan. He was a powerful man and had many friends around him. Every year he would go on a journey to see some new place, sometimes by boat and sometimes by land. Now this particular year, O'Lorcan decided to go by boat, and so he set about preparing his three-sail gleoiteog boat and his crew for his journey. It was going to be a long journey around Ireland, and he had never done that distance before. He had to arrange for stores and provisions to be loaded for the trip.

As he was nearing Achill Island, he could see that there was a storm brewing behind him. Eventually, the storm overtook them, and it was the worst storm he had ever experienced. They had to run before the storm for some time, but finally they were not able to manoeuvre well and the storm pushed them in to the shore on Inishturk.

There was a man and his family living on Inishturk by the name of Thady O'Toole. One morning after a great storm had hit the island and was still blowing hard, Thady was out dressed in his usual frieze clothing tending to his sheep, and he saw that a boat had landed on the strand below with its sails all in tatters. When he went down to examine the boat, he saw that there was a man and his crew there in miserable condition, having been almost drownded. He brought them all up to his house, fed them and let them rest. O'Lorcan stayed there with O'Toole for eight days and eight nights while they were weather-bound by the storm. Every morning for the eight days, Thady would go out and kill a fresh sheep. By the ninth day the wind was reduced, and the weather was favourable. O'Lorcan and his crew had meanwhile fixed up the sails and mast as they were always waiting for better weather to sail home in. When they were finally leaving, O'Lorcan asked O'Toole to come visit him in Meath the following summer.

When the next summer came, O'Toole decided that he might as well go to Meath. He prepared himself for the long journey and took off to go all the way to Meath. When he landed there, he went to the back door of O'Lorcan's castle and knocked on the door. An usher came on down and asked him what did he want. O'Toole said he wanted to see the Chieftain O'Lorcan. The usher went upstairs and said to the chieftain that there was a man in frieze clothing at the back door wanting to see him. Now, O'Lorcan was in the midst of entertaining for dinner a great party of other chieftains. When O'Lorcan heard from the usher that there was a man in frieze apparel, he knew very well it was O'Toole of Inishturk that was there. He quickly went down to the back door, took him by the two hands, brought him up to his dining hall and placed him sitting at the head of the table.

It was a great wonder to the other chieftains there that O'Lorcan had put a man with a frieze coat at the head of his table. They didn't understand it at all, and they started grumbling against O'Lorcan, but when he heard their remarks, he begged their pardon and explained that he, the O'Lorcan, was treated better on Inishturk than he was in his own house in Meath.[37]

Turf competition, Bog of Allen, Co. Kildare, 1937.

CHAPTER 6

Rural Life and Tradition

⌘

Dispute About Owning the Foal

THIS STORY UNFOLDED OUT ON the mountain in the area around Glenkeen. There were two men from not too far from there in the village of Srahrevagh, and they were the best of friends and neighbours for years. They both had the common grazing for their two mares up on the mountain by Glenkeen. Now it happened that the two mares were due to foal in the month of May. Perhaps one of the mares got sick at the time of foaling. Anyway, one of them went near the brink of a cliff when she was due to foal. Just at the time of foaling, didn't an eagle come over her as she foaled, and didn't the eagle startle the mare, and the foal hurtled on down over the cliff 'til he got stuck on a little branch and wasn't he killed by the fall. The two mares went on with their lives, and they both took to suckling the one foal. When the owners heard of there being only one foal, they went out to the mountain to see what had happened, and didn't they find one dead foal and one foal being well cared for by the two mares.

Now these two good friendly neighbours began to dispute the ownership of the living foal.

'This foal is my foal,' says the one.

'No, 'tis my foal,' says the other.

The row began in earnest 'til they almost went to murder one another. They were striking and fighting each other and using the worst names for each other. Finally, they agreed that they should go to the court and have the court settle the question as to which of them owned the foal while each of the mares were giving him a tit. The magistrate couldn't decide, and he sent the case to the higher court. When the higher judge heard the case, he couldn't decide it either, and he said he'd send it out to the parish priest to decide.

'How in the world can I decide it?' says the priest.

As it happened there was an old man in the village, Martin Madden (Mairtín Ó Madhan), and he heard of the dispute going on over the foal and that neither the judges nor the priest could decide.

'I'll decide it,' says Martin. He told the two men, 'Bring the two mares and the foal down to the river on the next Monday.'

Now on the Monday afternoon, the two men were down by the river with the mares and the foal, and everyone in the county around gathered to see how Martin would decide this difficult dispute.

'Well,' says he, 'let you both bring your mares to the edge of the water and then you both take the foal and thrust him out in to the water. Whichever mare of them owns the foal will go down in to the water for him.'

The men thrust the foal out in to the river, and the next thing was that one of the mares was down on her two knees on the brink of the river reaching out to pull the foal in while the other mare went off grazing, helping herself and never looked at the colteen. The two neighbours accepted the decision, and the dispute was settled, and they remained good friends and neighbours.

Since that time the place where the foal was thrown in has been called Poll a Capaill or Hole of the Horse. It's above the bridge on the Carrownisky River in Srahrevagh at Glenkeen.[1]

꙳

Mrs Jordan's First Sickness

One day me mother says to me, 'Jamsie, in about eight days' time, I won't be any trouble to you any longer.'

Me mother was a formidable woman and had lived through a lot and was well respected. Any of the local priests that would pass nearby on the island would never pass out without coming to see her for she was blind, and they knew it. When she wanted them to hear her confession, I'd send them word and ready the house for them, and they'd come.

I was very pleased when she died that nothing untoward happened to her during her blind time. Many's the time I thought of her when I was working abroad in England and my foot on a spade on someone else's land. I'd leave the work there and come home with my hands behind my back to look after her if she needed it.

Me mother never had a doctor in her life nor any of the whole family. We never knew anything about doctors. We were a very sound people.

She had developed a cough and a sort of dry windy turn in her stomach. She says one day, 'James, you go to the doctor and see about me.'

'Alright,' says I.

I went in to Westport and Doctor Birmingham was a well-known local doctor there at the time. He was an old man about sixty years or over and a strange man that had come to Westport only a year or two before. So, I went to the doctor's office and knocked. 'Twas on a Friday and about ten years before she died. She'd be a good hearty woman then. When this old man, Dr Birmingham, opened the door and says, 'Well, my man, what do ye want?'

I says, 'Me mother is not feeling well, and I came to see if you could prescribe a remedy to cure her.'

'What's your mother's name,' says he.

'She's Ellen Jordan of Inishnakillew,' says I.

'Well,' say he, 'who is her doctor?

'Well,' says I, 'I never knew her to be attended by a doctor or anyone of the family.'

'It's a very good job for you,' says the doctor. 'Well now, how does she feel?'

'Well,' says I, 'she takes a turn in her stomach, doctor, and it's more of a dry turn than anything else, like wind, and her mouth has a very heavy yellow blanche on it inside the roof of her mouth.'

'What age is she?' asks he.

'Well,' says I, 'she's over sixty anyways.'

'Well. Oh, well,' says he, 'we'll build her up this time, and she'll be alright.' He went and wrote out a prescription for him and came back to the door, and he says, 'Go to the chemist now with that, and he'll put it right for you.'

'What chemist will l go to?' says l for there were two of them in Westport at the time.

'Go to Stack's Chemist,' says he, 'for the old drugs are worth nothing. They're no good.' Stack was a young man who had recently set up his shop in Westport.

Before l left, l says, 'Doctor, for what am l in your debt now?'

'You owe me nothing,' says he, 'but the people of Kilmeena i'd be better off if they troubled Dr Birmingham more often than they do.'

'Well,' says l, 'surely, and what about the roof of the mouth for this blanche?'

'It's all coming from the stomach,' says the doctor, 'and as the stomach goes right that'll clear away by itself.'

l went to Stack's Chemist with the prescription and gave it to him. He looked at it. 'It'll be an hour,' says he, 'before I'll have this ready for you.'

'Well,' says l, 'it might be worth it.' l jobbed about the place and did the business that l had to do and returned within the hour. Stack then says, 'It'll be another half an hour or twenty minutes more.' So, l went off again and returned on time.

'l have it ready now for you, Mr Jordan,' says Stack.

'Very well,' says l, 'and what's the price?'

'Three shillings and eight pence.'

'Well,' says l, 'it ought to be good for that price for I'm long enough waiting for it.'

'Well, it's the best drug that l ever mixed, and your doctor is a good doctor.'

'Thank you, sir,' says l, and l gave him the money and walked out and brought it home.

Me mother used it up, the drug, according to the instructions, and she never ailed again for a day 'til the day she died. He was a good doctor, surely. He had good timber to work on for he knew she never had a doctor before. When one has good timber to work with, one can give it a good back of the hatchet, and it won't fly far off. There's nothing to beat good timber or good stuff.[2]

⁓

The Old Woman Who Knew the Past and the Future

One day I was churning me butter in the house. It was a pretty cold day, and this old lady was walking along the road and came up to the door of the house, and I says to her, 'Come in to the house, pull up to the fire, and warm yerself.'

'God bless,' says she as she was coming in, and she sat down in the corner of the fire. 'And would ye have a graineen of tobacco on ye?'

I went over and gave her about the size of a pipe full. She put it in her pipe, and with a sod from the fire, she lit the pipe and had a smoke.

When she had enough smoked, she began praying like to herself.

'God bless,' says she, 'you have a good heart. You gave me all the tobacco you had.'

'How did you know that,' says I, 'for that was the truth? I was preparing to go to town, and I wouldn't make two halves of the small amount of tobacco as I was going to get some more in the town.'

She told me a lot of things that had happened to me before that. She was psychic.

'You're getting ready to go to town now,' says she, 'and when you go to town, you'll meet two men, and they'll try to force your hand to take a drink, but don't take it,' says she. 'Don't take it.'

I went to town and met the two men. I knew them well, and indeed they tried to force me to take a drink. Well, I had a pint poured and had it up to me mouth, but I put it down and walked out. Psychology goes a long way![3]

❧

The Writing That Drove Out the Rats

One evening a poor woman landed up to the door of this house, and she had a couple stone of potatoes in a bag on her back with her. She asked for lodgings of them, and they up and told her, they would give her lodging and welcome, and they asked if she wouldn't have a bit in her bag that the rats would have eaten by the morning.

'I've got a husband,' she says, 'that will banish the rats from you. He's gone up that road beyond,' she says, 'to the villages up at the hill, and he promised to meet me here to-night when we were parting on the road beyond.'

'Well, if that's the cure, a chuisle,' says she, 'we'll give you lodging and welcome.'

So, she got ready a bit to eat for herself, and when she had that eaten, the night was coming on. By night fall, who landed in to them but her husband.

'There's an awful state here in this house,' the wife says to the husband. 'These people that I'm into the house here with.'

'What's the matter with them?' says he.

'They're plagued by a swarm of rats,' says she, 'and I up and told them,' says she, 'that you'd do away with the rats by me getting lodging here for the night.'

'Well, yes,' says he. 'When I've had me supper, I'll prepare meself for that job. Let ye put down a pot of potatoes,' says he, 'if ye have them, and when they're done, let ye spill them out on a basket.'

The pot of potatoes was put on, and when they were boiled, they were spilt out on a basket, and he was beyond at the table writing a bit of a note at the time.

'And let ye take them now,' says he, 'and spread them out under the beds, and let ye place this note on top of them under the first bed that ye started with and remember,' says he, 'that I'm going to send them to somewhere where they have something to eat in it.'

The woman of the house talked with her husband, and she says, 'Send them to Leanley's corn mill, behind at Tully, near Srahrevagh, outside Louisburgh.'

As soon as they had everything ready, he says, 'Let ye go and open the back door and front door and room door.' As soon as the doors were opened, it wasn't long 'til the rats landed down, with the first big rat leading them. They called her the Owner Rat, and she had the paper in her mouth, and it would shock you to hear the cry of them coming down from the room to them, and there's not a rat of them but all had a potato in his mouth, and the last of them had the biggest potato of the lot with him. That Leanley and his mill had the herd of the rats until people gave up bringing corn to his mill. The whole village of Tully was swarming with rats for a year after that, and no one knows what became of them from that day to this.[4]

⌇

Bone Setter

Geraghty was a bone setter in Aillemore, near Louisburgh. He had books, stories and rhymes for the whole world, and he was good for healing pleurisy, doing farming or anything else.

Geraghty could get twelve eggs, let them down between his hands, and throw back their yolks but kept the egg-whites in a bowl to help with the setting. He would take a piece of white flannel and work it well into the egg-whites. He could set a bone with his thumb whilst his other hand was held down. To fix a broken bone, he would prepare four good kippers, bind the flannel lightly round, put down the kippers and wind more flannel around.

Once, he bent a man's arm, put it in a sling, and he never felt any pain.

When Geraghty was living in Aillemore, he was once sought out because I, then only aged three, had lost me eyesight. 'I can't see me hand,' says I to me mother, and she dropped down on the floor. Geraghty came over right away and helped the situation.

On another occasion I had hurt my arm and hand seriously, broken some of the bones, and Geraghty was called in. The bone was sticking out above the elbow. Geraghty got the egg-whites, the flannel, the kippers, and applied them all to me hand. A week late he loosened the flannel and told me to exercise me hand. He explained to me how to do some exercises for me hand and arm would build back power in the muscle. Blisters appeared on me finger, and he was able to set that finger also.[5]

✦

The Land That Was Hard on a Hare

When people applied for a pension, the application was submitted to a pension administration in Dublin, but it had to be reviewed by a committee of local people and a local pension officer in the area where the applicant was from.

In early 1940 there was an old man from Boheh, near Glenbaun on the other side of Croagh Patrick, who had applied for a pension for ten shillings, but the pension officer in Westport would allow him only four shillings. The man had to appear before the pension committee in person, and he was expecting to get himself the full ten shillings. The committee felt that he was too well off, and that he shouldn't get so much of a pension.

The parish priest, who was on the committee, said that he'd favour allowing him eight shillings. However, the man said that as long as God left him life for his pension, he should be entitled to the full pension.

'Well,' says he to the priest, 'you're a servant of God, and it'll be before God you'll appear when you go to him, and surely he will see and remember what you've been trying to do to me here today.'

The priest said again that he would recommend the man get only the eight shillings.

Then a member of the audience who was allowed into the committee hearing, Pat Máille, stood up and says, 'He's not well off at all, and it's terrible bad land that he has out there in Boheh, and he should have the full pension.'

'That's true enough, aggrah,' says the old man. 'It'd give a hare a heart burn to walk on it, the grass was so poor.'

The committee had another discussion about his application and awarded him the full ten shillings. The old man was sitting there in his bawneen, which he wore on even the warmest day of the year, and he was pleased with himself.[6]

The House That Couldn't Keep a Cock

In me aunt's house, they couldn't keep a cock. She lived beside me mother, and the two houses were both joined together, and they are this side of the castle of Castleaffy, near Roscahill.

One day a traveller passed by the house, an unknown man, and he came in to them to the house. When he seen the cock there, he says, 'You keep a very good cock.'

'Oh, we do,' says me aunt, 'but it's a very short while we can keep any one cock, but we're keeping this one for sure.'

'Well,' says he, 'you have this one long enough and don't have him long now. Company has passed through this house many a night, and the cock makes an awful alarm,' and he was right too.

'That's true enough, for sure,' me aunt says.

'And you have a habit of leaving pots and skillets out back by the back door,' says he, 'straightening up the house before ye go to bed. Well,' says he, 'in the future leave them out by the wall at the front of the house so they will be out of the way. That back door does be opened when you don't hear it, and the front door too. Be advised now by me, and do as I say,' says he, 'and goodbye to ye.'

Me uncle, me aunt's husband, was up on roof of the house. It was a stormy night. He heard a child crying as he was making a scallop in his hand to fix the roof sticking it down to keep the thatch from being blown away. He came down out off the roof immediately and still heard a child crying in the air near him. After they complied with all the travelling man's regulations about organising the pots and pans, they never had no more trouble.[7]

⤲

Andrew Moore Goes to the Fairy Dance in Newport

The Moores had lived on Inishoo for a long time. They were very jolly, decent men and were known as great amusers with music. One day Andrew Moore rowed into Newport, which was the local market town, to do some business. When his business was done and it was duskish, he went down the quay to his small boat to come home. He was getting to the boat, and didn't he meet a man he didn't know on the quay.

'Good night, Andrew,' says he.

'Good night, yerself,' says Andrew.

'Isn't it early yet to be going home?' said the young man.

'It'll be late enough for me,' says Andrew, 'when I'll be beyond in Inishoo.'

'Come with me,' says the young man, 'and I'll bring you to a great dance tonight.'

Andrew thought having a little merriment wouldn't be a bad idea at all and went along with him. Before they had gone about twenty yards, Andrew was landed in to a fine mansion where there was music and light, and the whole place filled with youngsters of the finest class of people going, both girls and boys. He took no notice but went along and engaged himself. There was a welcome from everyone in their turn for Andrew Moore.

It wasn't long until one of them approached him. 'Here, Andrew, tune up this fiddle to your taste.' Andrew, who was a good fiddler, took the fiddle and drew the bow down, you understand if you knows how to sound a fiddle.

'What's it going to be, Andrew?' says the fellow.

'Oh, a double jig,' says Andrew.

'Then give us "Geese in the Bog".' Andrew went on with the 'Geese in the Bog', and this fellow who gave him the fiddle and another man went out on the floor, and they did a fairly good dance for a double jig. After that dance was over, someone called Andrew to see if he could do anything like that. Andrew and another man went out on the floor, and there was more shouting for Andrew all over the house when he had his jig danced. When Andrew had his night in and enjoyed it well with girls and youngsters and all, the man from the quay took him back to the door.

'Now, Andrew Moore, it's time for you to be going home,' says he.

When Andrew looked round, he saw no more of the mansion nor a one that was in it. He was there all alone on the quay. He went down in to his boat, pulled off his coat, took his two oars and pulled until he come to Inishgowla. When he come to Inishgowla, didn't Walter O'Malley of Inishcoife see the boat coming in in the morning.

'Good morning, Andrew,' says he, 'and ye must have had a great night of it in Newport to be coming home so now.'

'Well, I had,' says Andrew, and he up and tells the whole tale to his comrade Walter.[8]

An Fear Gorta

Me daddy, when he was a young man, and me mammy was married to him then, bought a cow at the Westport fair from a man by the name of David Brown of Seaview, near Kilmeena. After the fair, himself and me mammy were coming home to Inishnakillew, and it happened to be evening when they got as far as Lishen Ruadh in Rossakeeran, near Moyna, and begorra, he suddenly got weak, and he called on her for help to keep him from falling.

'William,' says she, 'what's wrong with you?'

'Well,' says he, 'I don't know, but I've lost the walk.'

She often told me that she never got it harder than to bring him from there to Claggan. His legs gave from under him in Claggan, up above by Willie Gibbons' house. She went in to Gibbons and told him what was the trouble. She was a young woman at the time and didn't know what was wrong.

'You have an féar gorta, boy,' says Gibbons, the minute me daddy went in and sat down. Gibbons went over to the cupboard, and there was a bageen of oatmeal within.

'Here,' says he, 'hold out your hand,' and he held his hand out and some of the oats dropped in to his hand. 'Eat on that and chew it well,' and he threw the rest of it in the fire. They remained there 'til they had their supper, and then they walked in here to Inishnakillew with their cow comfortable and hearty.[9]

An Féar Gorta on the Roads

On occasion a sudden attack of an féar gorta can occur and can be a surprise to a man when travelling along parts of mountains or rural roads. When a man goes through these places, he'd be attacked by such a kind of weakness or hunger, and he's often unable to walk any further. The cure then is for him to eat any sort of food. He could even chance to chew on a piece of a whang or leather or leather shoelace from his shoe or chew a bit of a certain kind of grass or heather.

Once this man was visiting in a house in Carrowmore and a man, by the name of Mick Ward, who was there, told the man that on his way home one time, he was overcome by an féar gorta on the Leenaun Road, and he had to sit down. Luckily for him, he was able to get a bit of heather that was growing on the side of the road. He picked it, chewed on it, and he was able to get up again and continue on as he was all right again. It seems it leaves no evil effects at all after it.[10]

⁂

The Oats That Were Threshed on the Church Floor

Back in the summer of 1883, the landlord of Clare Island wanted to make sure that the islanders would pay him what was due him, and knowing that a principal source of island revenue came from the sale of the crops, mainly the oats, the landlord sent out to Clare a contingent of police to watch over the crops on the land until they were ready to be saved. The police stayed in various houses around the island. There were twelve police and two sergeants out there as well as two men from the Burns family and two emergency men.

Now, the islanders had a meeting to consider what they should do about the crops so they could save them for themselves. They decided to arrange to invite all the police in to MacCabe's pub and give them plenty of drink on a Sunday, when there would be no one working in the fields on the island. Meanwhile, the islanders all gathered and spread out to cut the crops, bring the wheat in to the chapel and thresh the wheat there on the floor of the church. It was all done in a few hours and the whole place was cleaned out, but all the crops had been saved, and the landlord got none of them. The police only found out what had happened the next day, and they had to return to the mainland in disrepute. A complaint was made by the landlord to the local parish priest in Westport.

In due course after this story escalated, Archbishop McEvilly of Tuam came out to the island to review the situation. Father Quinn, the local parish priest, who had allowed the islanders to use the church, was severely reprimanded by the Archbishop and later would be sent to America. Canon Grealy from Newport was sent in to replace Fr Quinn, but he was so insulting and abusive to the people that he was soon removed and shifted from there to Achill. Father Burke, Fr William Joyce from Louisburgh, and William O'Brien, MP, were all involved that day helping the people out, and they too were sent off the island.

Sometime later there was a confirmation service being held in Louisburgh with Archbishop McEvilly attending, and Fr Quinn appeared at the confirmation without having been properly invited as he knew the people. The Archbishop noticed that Fr Quinn was present without a proper invitation. Fr Quinn admitted that he was not officially invited, but he said that he had come to ask leave of His Grace to go to America, and it was granted. He went out then to America to a place, Cleveland, Ohio. He would come home on a visit occasionally.[11]

‡

The Man Who Left a Good Fire Behind Him

Many years ago, there was over two hundred fifty houses in Westport built out of sods and every kind of an ould lump of stone they could gather. A group of men would start building a sod-house in the morning and would be finished building by the evening.

Once on a pretty cold night in the early spring, this ould fellow put down a pretty good fire to warm himself in his sod-house. At the time all the little sod-houses were quite dry. When the ould fellow started his fire, didn't sparks from his sod-house spread to some other sod-houses, and there was a great uncontrollable blaze going within ten minutes. All the inhabitants had to flee as their houses were on fire, and, for sure, they wanted to know how and where the fire had started. When they heard that the ould man's sod-house had started it, they all made to charge after him. He knew they would kill him if they got hold of him. He made off out the Leenaun road. When he got as far as Knappagh, he went up to a house there as he was trying to get his breath after the threat of abuse he had received, and he sat down near the door.

The man of the house says to him, 'Come on in, pull up to the fire, man, and warm yourself as the night is cold.'

'Throth, I'm not cold, but I left a good fire after me where I left.'

In ten days' time, he went back again to Westport and found that the whole section of sod-houses in the town had been rebuilt except his own little house.[12]

⌇⌇⌇

Country Games Near Louisburgh

<u>Handball:</u> There was a handball alley at Gowlaun on the road between Killeen and Tallybaun. There were several other alleys

built out of gables through the half parish, but Gowlaun was the oldest one. The ball used to play handball was made of woollen yarn, doubled and wound hard around with a small piece of cork in the centre until it was the size of the standard solid ball and then covered with tanned sheepskin. The sheepskin was cut in squares and then a shoemaker covered the ball. That sort of ball gave a good hop, but it was not as lively as a solid which was so hard that it would nearly break your hand, and so they hit it lightly.

Throwing stones: Stones would be thrown from the shoulder. They were mostly round and oblong and weighed about twenty-eight pounds. The first stone would be flung down the road as far as one could, and then the next fellow followed him. The one with the least number of throws over the course would be the winner. The course might be over a mile long.

Weight lifting: One of the games was a competition to lift a big stone, the heaviest that could be found, and then throw it as far as one could. The same stone would then be used by the other competitors.

Hop-step and jump: This game of jumping on one's feet was often played in the bog in summertime when they were turf cutting. It was a feat of jumping.

Wake games: They would make a hard solid sugan, then double it, and knot one end of it. It was called a brogue. They'd sit in a circle and a lot would be drawn as to who'd stand in the centre of the circle. The brogue would be passed quickly from player to player under their knees. If the man in the centre managed to intercept the brogue as it was passed, then the player who had just passed the brogue would have to go in the centre. Perhaps there was a musical element to the game, 'Hart a Broeg', which was played as the brogue was being passed and then the music stopped and a ditty was sung.

MacMuerrheue: This was a way where one could take out one's spite on a man if he was after your girl.

Game of the palm of the hand: A man would bend his back and place his hands behind his back. The other man would hit the palm of his hand three to five times; sometimes he would play until the blood came out. The second player could settle the first player in any position he liked. After that, the players would change places.

Match making: Sometimes if a boy and girl would be courting, an arrangement would be made by a match maker so that the couple could be married. The match maker handled the negotiations between the two families, and it was a position of distinction in the community.[13]

Road to Doolough, near Louisburgh, Co. Mayo, 1938.

Afterword on Ernie
O'Malley's Folklore

꠸ᨮ

ERNIE O'MALLEY'S FOLKLORE COLLECTION ANSWERED a long-standing call to preserve a tradition that was in steady decline. Between 1917 and 1923 folklorist Thomas Johnson Westropp commented on the challenges of being an 'occasional visitor' to the region and regretted that 'the work ... had been better done by dwellers on that wild coast; but few indeed show interest in such a pursuit, and the old Ireland is passing away forever, more and more speedily.'[1] This pessimistic view about the fate of Ireland's oral tradition persisted even after the establishment of An Cumann le Béaloideas Éireann (The Folklore of Ireland Society) in 1927, the government-backed Institiúid Bhéaloidas Éireann (Irish Folklore Institute) in 1930, and finally, the formidable Coimisiún Béaloideasa Éireann (Irish Folklore Commission) in 1935. Séamus Ó Duilearga, a pivotal figure in all three organisations and in developing collectors' preservation guidelines, spoke as late as 1945 of the 'pressing need' for the 'systemic and active collection of the oral traditions of the peoples of the world'. Despite the Commission's progress, he reflected that the day was soon approaching 'when the sources of tradition will have dried up in the drifting sands of progress, and the voice of the story-teller and tradition-bearer will be stilled for ever'.[2]

Five years earlier, and over twenty years after Westropp had lamented the inevitable imposition of modernity on rural Ireland, O'Malley began gathering folklore around Clew Bay.[3] After two years of these late-night storytelling sessions (1940–42), O'Malley had collected 330 pieces of folklore from twenty-six local tellers. This book offers a selection of those stories.

O'Malley's material reflects and indeed anticipates the topics included in Seán Ó Súilleabháin's foundational collectors' guide, *A Handbook of Irish Folklore* (1942), which was published just as O'Malley was completing his fieldwork. It is hardly surprising that O'Malley's collections – covering historical characters, the lore of fairies, places and the sea, hero tales and country life – reflect many of the popular categories marked out by Ó Súilleabháin and the National Folklore Collection. On return trips to Dublin from his family home at Burrishoole Lodge, near Newport, he mingled with a wide-ranging crowd of writers and intellectuals, including Ó Duilearga, and would have been aware of the most recent trends within the Commission and in the field more generally.[4]

In a letter to Eithne Golden in 1940, he outlined his efforts to collect 'a good deal of history, stories and miscellaneous material ... from people around this Bay'.[5] O'Malley invited the US-based Golden to visit Mayo, and offered to teach her the technique for collecting so that she might, in turn, collect folklore among Irish emigrant communities in America. O'Malley stressed that such lore had to be recorded and 'should eventually be used to supplement the Folklore Commission here [in Ireland]'.[6] His desire to see the Commission's impact stretch to the diaspora is significant and was likely informed by his own experiences abroad. During this time, he encountered many former comrades who had left as part of the exodus of republican activists following the Civil War. Similarly, in his formative *On Another Man's Wound* (1936), O'Malley recalled varied experiences of listening to islanders' experiences abroad, first as a child amongst the men of Achill Island, who 'talked around the turf fires of their hardships and adventures in foreign ports', and later as an IRA organiser on the Aran islands, where returned emigrants told 'strange' stories of American cities like Boston and Philadelphia.[7] The tales in *The Enchanted Bay* are peppered with references to Clew Bay's own strong emigration history, particularly between Achill Island and Cleveland, Ohio.

O'Malley saw his own efforts to preserve Clew Bay's lore as supplementary to the work of the Commission. He proclaimed that the Commission's material was amongst the most important collections in Europe and anticipated that it would become an important 'repository for creative work', because of the universal appeal of its myths and legends.[8] O'Malley's recognition that Irish folklore was transferable between cultures and that it had a potential role in future creative output, rather than being confined to a national past, helps to explain a seeming contradiction – between the modernism with which O'Malley is often associated and the perceived parochialism of Irish folklore as part of the post-partition state-building project.

For O'Malley, folklore formed part of what Diarmuid Ó Giolláin referred to as 'a world view alternative to the official conception of the world'. In this way, it was essential to both the ongoing process of decolonisation and resistance to undesirable aspects of the new state.[9] David Lloyd picks up on this dynamic in his assessment of O'Malley's intellectual career, commenting that his interests lie 'not in the modernization of Ireland, understood in accord with capitalist modernization internationally, but in an alternative modernity that seeks to assert its difference'.[10] As such, for O'Malley, the folk tradition was integral to the development of an independent Irish creative consciousness.

***

In an influential address to An Cumann le Béaloideas Éireann in 1977, Bo Almqvist reflected upon the achievement and legacy of the Irish Folklore Commission. He recalled how early collectors had won the trust of the many people whose doors they had darkened and noted how they were never 'mistaken for tax collectors, gunmen on the run, or whatever else a stranger in an area can be mistaken for'.[11] Ironically, it was O'Malley's early experience as an IRA organiser, traversing the countryside on his bicycle and relying on the hospitality of local sympathisers, that laid the foundation for his lifelong interests in folklore and documenting the sociocultural landscapes around him.

While O'Malley was immersed in Mayo's lore from an early age, when his family moved to Dublin in 1906 he was then exposed to the trappings of Anglo-American mass culture. He later recalled: 'We told our school chums stories of Fionn and Cuchulain, but they laughed at us. They had read the latest Buffalo Bill, could talk of the red varmints of Indians, Colt-emptying frontier fighters, of split-up-the-back Eton suits and the rags of that other public-school life of the *Magnet* and *Gem*. Only to ourselves now did we talk about the older stories.'[12]

Yet upon his travels across the country, particularly the West, as a grassroots republican organiser, O'Malley rekindled his appreciation for what might be described as an alternative cultural landscape, rooted firmly in local myth, history and lore. Indeed, O'Malley recalled that as he built up an army along the darkened backroads of rural Ireland, the fear of supernatural places like earthen 'fairy' forts, and beings like the mythic Black Pig near Strokestown, or the demonic, eight-foot shadowy hand of west Clare, appeared as real a threat to the solo traveller as the prospect of British patrols.[13]

This connection between the supernatural and the extraordinary circumstances of the revolutionary period was by no means unique.[14] The accounts of the Bureau of Military History hold testimonies of former combatants that are littered with similar references to everything from local revered sites and figures to aspects of the otherworldly. In one example, an IRA officer recalled how he and a comrade became disoriented and stuck in a field in the Dublin mountains despite their deep knowledge of the area. The IRA officer's mother and other older locals later explained that they: 'had disturbed the Good People (meaning Fairies) and by sitting down you had broken the spell and your way was clear'.[15] In another more humorous example, Belfast volunteer Ailbhe Ó Monacháin, or Alf Monaghan, recalled how he and two comrades 'nearly revived the [local] belief in fairies – if it ever died out' when they took to footing the locals' turf during their nightly activities when on the run in rural County Clare.[16] Meanwhile in west Connemara, IRA officer Martin Conneely relayed how he once cheekily told a non-local comrade that the lonesome outpost they occupied was 'haunted, that "fairies" were seen there'.[17]

The Enchanted Bay's stories are rife with similar local phenomena. The collection contains a wealth of fairy lore. These range from otherworldly sightings and the occasional warning or message to stories of changelings and other mischievous happenings. The stories also reflect supernatural connections to the land and seascapes, including the '*féar gortach*' (hungry grass), a cursed patch of land that brings an insatiable hunger to anyone unfortunate enough to step on it, the '*ceo draíochta*' (fairy mist), a sudden, disorienting fog, and the misfortune that befell the young IRA officer in the Dublin mountains, the '*fóidín mearbhaill*' (disorienting sod), a patch which similarly causes confusion and leads one astray.[18] These phenomena formed part of broader beliefs associated with 'lonesome places' which, Dáithí Ó hÓgáin tells us, had a 'combined mystical and menacing nature' causing them 'to be regarded with a degree of awe'.[19]

Communal resistance and resilience feature as a common thread in the stories, capturing how Clew Bay's residents survived against the backdrop of harsh and unforgiving land and seascapes, political turmoil, and the region's many perceived supernatural elements. In many instances, the collection also reflects the degree to which class struggle has long been at the heart of Irish society. One vignette set in the 1820s exemplifies this harsh reality: 'In those days, it was not unusual for a lad to go wandering off. There was no work for the lads locally, and so some of them just walked about looking for some place better. Some would join the military, others would look for work in the cities.'[20] In another powerful example from the height of the famine in 1847, a group of starving locals in Kilmeena are faced with military action for agitating against their landlord. Upon facing sure death at the hands of the authorities, the group agreed that it 'was as well for them to die fighting as to die starving of hunger.'[21]

However, one of the most striking examples of local resistance comes in a tale set in the early 1880s, in which the people of Clare Island fight off a process server seeking to issue evictions. Notably, in the two tellings of this story, his defeat is organised and carried out by a group of local women. This raises the question of gender as regards O'Malley's folklore. The Irish Folklore Commission did not employ any women as full-time collectors and also had an under-representation of female informants; so too, most of O'Malley's stories were collected from male tellers.[22] There was a general imbalance in folklore collecting at the time and Mícheál Briody notes that the 'antipathy towards women in Irish society, particularly in rural society, affected the number of women the Commission collected from as well as the amount and the nature of the material collected from them'.[23] Yet interestingly, as evidenced by the earlier letter to Eithne Golden, O'Malley hoped to enlist her help and to teach her the techniques for collecting. How, if he had succeeded, might this have impacted the material gathered?

Aspects of the female experience are captured in many of the tales, as evidenced by the story of the communal fight against the process server and several others, ranging from supernatural tales to other historical vignettes. In one particularly notable example from O'Malley's fieldnotes, an informant talks about the everyday hardships faced by women in rural Ireland, as he describes a local woman named Brigid Tiernan, who had survived the Famine. When asked why she never married the man whom she later courted, she says: 'I'd have married him, but I'd be afraid I'd die in childbirth.'[24] In a similarly memorable story contained in this volume, another informant, Jamsie Jordan, recalls the eviction of his widowed mother, Ellen Coyne Jordan, in 1877.[25]

The lore collected by O'Malley also depicts well-known historical events like the French landing north of Killala in 1798 and local involvement in Fenianism during the mid-1800s – constituting what Guy Beiner describes as the 'often-neglected vernacular histories found outside the domains of mainstream professional historiography'.[26] At times, unlikely protagonists emerge, alongside unexpected storylines that don't fit neatly with the view of mid-twentieth-century Ireland as a conservative, Catholic state. This is particularly true of tales relating to local religious matters; informants tell of instances of interdenominational cooperation – a priest lending his congregation to a sparsely attended Protestant church to save a minister's job and a last-minute intervention from another Protestant minister to save the life of a doomed local Fenian.[27] Given O'Malley's unpublished literary depiction of refugees from the Belfast pogroms of 1922, another historical vignette, that of John Dennis Browne of Westport, is particularly intriguing.[28] The informant reveals how, amongst a slew of other more unfavourable actions, Browne, the 3rd Earl of Altamont, was remembered locally for his decision to 'build a new town in 1795' for Catholic refugees 'escaping from the sectarian conflict in the north of Ireland'.

Recalling his time as an IRA organiser in west Clare, O'Malley conveys how these vernacular histories inherently shaped the world view of rural communities: 'My guides at night told me bloodthirsty tales as we crossed the country; they knew what happened at each crossroads. Here a peeler, land-grabber, agent or landlord had been attacked or killed. Houses yet kept steel shutters from the days when a landlord's house was held in a state of siege, and when they wore suits of mail. Police in huts still guarded land-grabbers'.[29]

***

As Cormac O'Malley notes in his reflection at the start of this volume, despite his father's great efforts to preserve aspects of Clew Bay's folk tradition, his folklore collection lay idle and unread for decades. Despite sidelining his work as a collector when he moved on to other intellectual pursuits, there is evidence to suggest that he was eager to publish the material.[30] This volume represents the eventual realisation of that aim and, as such, is of great importance. Over one hundred years after Thomas Johnson Westropp bemoaned the rapid decline of the rich storytelling tradition in the West of Ireland, O'Malley's folklore collection, marked by his meticulous attention to detail, offers us unprecedented insight into the social and cultural tapestry of a coastal community that witnessed and endured some of the most pivotal events in modern Irish history.

Dr Patrick J. Mahoney

Standing stone, cairn and sacred site, Co. Mayo, 1938.

Editorial Notes

❧

I SHOULD MAKE SOME COMMENTS on the editing process through which these tales have gone. At this point only about 60 per cent of the original 330 tales have been transcribed, but based on many selection factors, only 111 are being published here. It was interesting to find that about fifteen of these tales are told in the first person, and they give the tales a sense of immediacy – of being present and listening to the speaker. Jamsie Jordan of Inishnakillew had most of these. To give some more background to the tales, I have added notes which include the name of each informant and the date when it was recounted. Sadly, I could find little biographical information about the informants, but perhaps more will be discovered. Though some tales go back to the eighteenth century or earlier, most reflect nineteenth-century experiences, but several tales relate to events as late as 1939–41. These later tales indicate how local lore was still used even then to explain events.

When I started to transcribe the Volume 6 notebook back in 1984, I knew that there had to be more notebooks in the series –

at least five more. It was not until 2014 that I was able to locate the additional notebooks (Nos 1–5, 7–12) in the National Folklore Collection with the help of Dr Críostóir Mac Cárthaigh. Then the transcription stage started, and over the years with a team of transcriber helpers, I transcribed over half of the tales. At that point, I wanted to see if they were of interest to people locally in Clew Bay and in folklore circles. With the help of a remarkable team of local men in the Newport–Westport–Castlebar area, Sean Cadden, Mick Mulchrone and Peter Mullowney, over the course of four years, I visited Newport regularly and we worked to correct the local spellings of surnames, place names, and vernacular words. Críostóir Mac Cárthaigh and Patrick J. Mahoney were most helpful with the expressions in Irish and their translation.

Most of the tales included in the book have been expanded slightly to give some introductory setting or context. Some explanatory words, for example relating to rural customs, have been added to give more colour to the events described. Days, months and numbers have been spelled out; ampersands (&) replaced by 'and'; g/f and g/m replaced by grandfather and grandmother; punctuation has been added to clarify the text. Most of Ernie's original vernacular words and their order within a sentence have been retained as this is the way they were spoken in the Clew Bay area where only Irish had been spoken up until relatively recently before the tales were collected. Ernie was not an Irish speaker and was not familiar with many local place names, and so wrote these down phonetically. The Irish he knew would have been that of the 1920s and not the modernised spelling. His handwriting is well known as being difficult and sometimes illegible, and so we have done our best with any word that was illegible.

In most cases the storyteller used present tense for dialogue with phrases such as 'says he', and that style has been retained. I have eliminated – but not lost – most of my father's original hundred local Clew Bay vernacular or phonetic words, such as 'wan' for 'one' or 'male' for 'meal' or 'sale' for 'seal' but have retained words such as 'drownded' or 'meself' which are still commonly used with a readily evident meaning. I have included a list of the original vernacular words below, which gives a sense of the local English dialect in the Clew Bay area at the time. My father's Irish was not good, and his phonetic writing was not always comprehensible, and so only some of the original Irish words remain along with his translation, as revised.

Some vernacular words have been changed but others have been retained. The list here gives some indication of the decisions made: **'again'** for 'agin', **'against'** for 'agin', **'anchor'** for 'ancker/ancher/anker', **'anchored'** for 'ankered', **'asked'** for 'axed', **'asking'** for 'axing', **'bade'** for 'bad', **'beat'** for 'bate/bet', **'beckon'** for 'bekon', **'breakfast'** for 'brekfast', **'breeze'** for 'braze', **'came'** for 'come', **'catch'** for 'ketch', **'clean'** for 'clane', **'cowed'** for 'coued', **'deal'** for 'dale', 'dealer' for 'daler', **'decent'** for 'dacent', retained **'didn't'**, **'doctor'** for 'docter', retained **'drownded'**, **'eat'** for 'ate', **'eaten'** for 'aten', **'eating'** for 'ating', **'floor'** for 'flure', **'fort'** for 'ft'/'firth', **'frieze'** for 'frise/fries/frith', **'gannet'** for 'gannett', **'had'** for 'has', **'halfpenny'** for 'hapenny', **'hare'** for animal 'hair', **'haunted'** for 'hunted', **'have'** for 'hav'/'ve', **'heart'** for 'hart', **'here'** for 'hare', **'hold'** for 'hould', **'in to'** not 'into', **'is'** for 'was', **'it would'** for 'i'd', **'jaundice'** for 'jaundis', **'jockey'** for 'jocket', **'leader'** for 'lader', **'leading'** for 'lading', **'leave'** for 'lave', **'linen'** for 'linnin', **'made'** for 'med', **'mane'** of horse for 'main', **'meal'** for 'male', **'meat'** for 'mate', **'march'** for 'marck', **'mesh'** for 'mash', **'mountain'** for 'mt', retained **'me'** for my and **'meself'** for myself, '**mutton**' for 'mutten', '**nearest**' for 'nearsed', '**never**' for 'n'er', '**oatmeal**' for 'oatmale', retained '**ould**' for old and '**ouldest**' for oldest, '**one**' for 'wan', '**partner**' for 'partener', '**pleased**' for 'plazed', '**potato/oes**' for 'pratie', retained '**poitin**' for poteen, '**read**' for 'red', '**rose**' for 'rises', '**raised**' for 'rose/ruz/riz', '**rigging**' for 'riggin', retained '**says**' for said, '**saw**' for 'seen', '**scents**' for 'sents', '**scholar**' for 'scoler', '**scolded**' for 'scoulded', '**sea**' for 'sgay', '**seal**' for 'sale', '**seaweed**' for 'sayweed', '**sung**' for 'sing', '**swept**' for 'swep', '**tea**' for 'tay', '**teach**' for 'tach', '**teacher**' for 'tacher', '**taught**' for 'learned', retained '**there'd**' for there would, retained '**there's**' for there are, retained '**they'd**' for there would, '**tilling**' for 'tileing', '**time**' for 'times', '**tongs**' for 'tongues', '**took**' for 'tak', '**us**' for 'uz', '**waistcoat**' for 'vestcoat', '**weave**' for 'wave', '**weaver**' for 'waver', '**weaving**' for 'waving', '**were**' for 'was', retained '**I'd**' for I would, '**wrack**' for 'rack', '**write**' for 'wrote', '**yeomen**' for 'yeos', retained '**ye**' for you, '**you're**' for 'yore', retained '**yer**' for your, retained '**yerself**' for yourself, retained '**you'd**' for you would.

The diminutive form of words has been retained as they can be readily understood; examples include: bageen, birdeen, boween, boyeen, calfeen, coleen, colteen, fireen, garsún (young boy), girleen, hageen, houseen, ladeen, lambeen, laneeen, pigeen, songeen and towneen.

Certain local expressions have been retained without explanation such as: acushla or a chuiscle, agrah or arragh, astura or astóir, begob, begorrah, be gorra, hangment, and troth.

Spellings of place names conform with www.logainm.ie, but commonly used names are referenced in the notes. Use was also made of www.townlands.ie.

Location of original interviews notebooks:

Vols 1–5 and Vols 7–12 are in the Ernie O'Malley Folklore Collection Notebooks, Box 1–3, at the National Folklore Collection ('NFC'), University College Dublin, Belfield, Dublin 4, Ireland.

Vol. 6 is in the Ernie O'Malley Papers, Archives of Irish America (AIA060), Series X, Box 15, Folder 18, Tamiment Library, New York University Library, 70 Washington Square, New York, NY 10012 U.S.A.

Interview Dates by Ernie O'Malley are presented in the footnote following each tale. He was out getting these tales on the following evenings around Clew Bay – principally the islands of Inishnakillew and Inishcottle, the Louisburgh area, but also Westport and other parts:

1940: twenty-seven nights: 2–3, 6–10, 12, 23–5, 28–9 February; 2–3, 5–9, 12, 14–15, 17, 24 March; 3 April; 11 November.

1942: Five nights: 24 March; 4, 26 April; 17, 26 May.

Standing stone near Killala, Co. Mayo, 1938.

Biographical Notes on Storytellers/Informants

Michael Gavin (1895–post-1940): Michael was a farmer from Inishbee. He was also involved in politics during the early days of the Clann na Talmhan (Children of the Soil) movement. Running on a platform of securing 'the rights that Davitt and Parnell gave' to the people, he stood in the local 1943 general election for Kilmeena district but was not elected. His tales are included on pages 131, 175.

John Geraghty (1864–post-1940): John was a farmer, originally from the seaside village of Lecanvey, between Westport and Louisburgh. He married his wife Margaret in 1901 and had five children. His tale is included on page 52.

James Jordan (*c.* 1866–post-1942): Jamsie, as he was known, was a farmer, born on the island of Inishnakillew. His father was William Jordan, son of Patrick Jordan, and he died prematurely in about 1869. His mother was Nellie or Ellen Coyne, who was born locally. They had four children. She was a cousin of John Nolan. Her Maille father had seven sons. James' father's mother, his grandmother, was Marie Haughey Maille, also from the island. Another Jordan grandfather had five sons. James' uncle was John Jordan who also lived on the island. His tales are included on pages 4, 20, 21, 23, 30, 35, 41, 43, 45, 46, 47, 50, 56, 57, 59, 60, 61, 62, 70, 77, 88, 92, 126, 134, 145, 151, 153, 157, 169, 177, 178, 180.

Thomas O'Brien (1880–post-1940): Tom was a farmer from Aghagower. His tales are included on pages 24, 26, 27, 29, 37, 38, 123, 128, 130, 146, 159, 162, 172, 183.

James O'Malley (1873–post-1940): Jim 'Badog' was a farmer originally from Caher, but he lived in the Louisburgh area. His tales are included on pages 5, 117, 150.

John O'Malley (1867–1964): John was originally from Carrowdaggan, but later lived in Bunowen, near Louisburgh. He was active in local politics from early on and was the first president of Sinn Féin for the Louisburgh district. His tales are included on pages 105, 156.

Michael O'Malley (1873–post-1940): Mickey was a farmer from Carrowmore, near Louisburgh. His brother, Martin, was born in 1879 and his sister Margaret in 1876. His tales are included on pages 6, 8, 9, 60, 91, 112, 137, 181.

Patrick O'Malley (1875–post-1940): Pat 'Round' was a mill clerk from Rossbeg, on the south shore outside Westport. His tales are included on pages 1, 3, 19, 29, 38, 67, 78, 87, 90, 106, 108, 109, 120, 133, 141, 184.

William O'Malley (1889–post-1940): William 'a Brich' was from Kilgeever, near Louisburgh. He lived with his widowed mother, Anne O'Malley. His maternal grandmother was Ellen McGloughlin of Glankeen who married William O'Malley. His tales are included on pages 14, 16, 72, 73, 80, 94, 101, 110, 135, 143, 167, 173.

James Charles O'Toole (1865–post-1940): Jamsie was a farmer originally from Aghany, near Roonah Quay just west of Louisburgh. In 1910 he married Mary O'Toole. The couple resided with his elderly parents before eventually taking over the family farm there. His tales are included on pages 10, 13, 53, 139, 142, 163, 182.

John O'Toole (1869–post-1940): John was originally from near the quay in Roonah, west of Louisburgh. He was a national schoolteacher in Louisburgh and lived there on Long Street for many years. His wife, Honoria, was from the village of An Cladach Dubh (Claddaghduff) near Omey Island in northwest Connemara. Like Clew Bay, that area was deeply impacted by both the Famine and intergenerational migration, particularly to the United States. The couple likely lived there for a time when first married in 1892, before eventually resettling in the Louisburgh area. Their first three of seven children were born in County Galway beginning in 1893. His tale in Vol. 4 (57) on the Clare Island drownings is slightly different to James Charles O'Toole's tale in Vol. 4 (24). His tales are included on pages 7, 8, 48, 54, 138, 154.

John Quinn (1871–post-1940): John was a farmer originally from the Gaeltacht village of An Caiseal (Cashel) on the east side of Achill Island. His grandfather was Michael Quinn but not related to the Quinns of Inishcottle. John's tales are included on pages 51, 113, 155.

Patrick Quinn (1856–1944): Patrick was a farmer from Inishcottle, as was his father, Michael (1821–post-1901). His son, Pat (1900–1980), lived on Inishcottle and married Nora Kelly of Islandmore. Pat's son, Paddy, still lives there and married Ann Jordan, the great-grandniece of James Jordan of Inishnakillew. Patrick's tales are included on pages 32, 33, 119, 176.

Carrigahowley Castle, Rockfleet, near Newport, Co. Mayo, 1975.

Acknowledgements

◦◦◦

MANY PEOPLE HAVE HELPED ME over the past forty years by transcribing, researching or just supporting my endeavours for these Clew Bay tales. My initial work started in 1984 when I discovered Volume 6 of my father's 1940 tales and started transcribing them. Dolores Delaney helped initially in Brussels. Justin Sammon of the Granuaile Centre in Louisburgh also tried. O'Malley Clan Chieftain Joe Blackwell and later Chieftain Ellen O'Malley Dunlop were most supportive. When Ellen recognised one tale about her grandfather, Anthony O'Malley, drowning off Clare Island, I realised that these tales related to real people with real stories. Chieftain Alice O'Malley of Chicago gave me great insights and a local map covering her family's Louisburgh area.

When in 2014 Críostóir Mac Cárthaigh, then director of the National Folklore Collection at University College Dublin, discovered ten more volumes of my father's tales, I also had to tackle them. Cliona de Paor gave me a great start with transcription. Fionnan MacGabhann gave me some help. Then Courtney Chambers from

Newport carried on. Edan McHugh of Achill helped one summer. Paul Michels, then of Islandmore, and Christy Barron gave me focus on island tales. Siobhan Kelly Gordon of Connecticut worked on transcription, research and editing. Eve Morrison and Anne Dolan offered technical assistance in coping with my father's writing. David Leeming of Stonington gave me a broad folklore perspective. Diarmuid Ó Giolláin and Pádraig Ó Siadhail were generous in giving me deeper insights into Irish folklore.

For the last few years, the local Mayo team of Peter Mullowney, Mick Mulchrone and Sean Cadden have been invaluable in supplying local knowledge for the area from the Killaries to Achill and abroad to Castlebar. We had long sessions in Newport trying to understand the local context of the tales and decide on their merits. Michael Cussack of Westport and Paddy Quinn of Inishcottle, a grandson of Patrick Quinn, one of the informants, joined us on several occasions. At Glucksman Ireland House, the New York University Center for Irish, Irish American and Global Studies, Marion R. Casey, Miriam Nyhan Grey, J.J. Lee and Kevin Kenny played a significant role in encouraging me to keep focused. Guy Beiner, director of Irish Studies at Boston College also encouraged me to persevere. Thanks to Rainer Kosbi for his maps and to Paula McGloin for her illustrations, and Conor Graham, Síne Quinn and all the team at Merrion Press.

The institutions holding the original tales, New York University Library with its Archives of Irish America (Shannon O'Neill) and the National Folklore Collection (Críostóir Mac Cárthaigh and Jonny Dillon) were fully supportive of these efforts.

I wish to acknowledge the generous support for this publication and overall project from the Glucksman Ireland House Advisory Committee at New York University.

ACKNOWLEDGEMENTS

I am indebted to my co-editor, Patrick J. Mahoney, who helped me to get these tales in publishable form and to get them off my desk to the readers.

Cormac K.H. O'Malley

Steps, Glendalough monastic site, Co. Wicklow, 1975.

Endnotes

❦

Reflections

1   *On Another Man's Wound* (Cork: Mercier Press, 2013), p. 15. His memoir was originally published in Dublin and London in 1936 and in the US in 1937 as *Army Without Banners* by Houghton Mifflin of Boston. There have been several other editions over the years.

2   *On Another Man's Wound* (henceforth *OAMW*), pp. 105–6.

3   *OAMW*, p. 123.

4   *OAMW*, p. 134.

5   Ella Young (1867–1956), Irish folklorist and mythologist, then living in California, had spent the summer with the wealthy arts patron Mabel Dodge Luhan (1879–1962), whose other guests that summer included Jean Marin, Georgia O'Keeffe, Becky Strand and others. See New Mexican Diaries, 29 September 1929, Ernie O'Malley Papers, in Archives of Irish America, New York University Library, New York ('EOM Papers AIA060'), Series X, Box 42, Folder 32.

6   These fictional writings are included in EOM Papers AIA060, Series I, Box 1, Folder 21 and Box 2, Folders 44 and 46.

7   See the non-folklore notebooks in Ernie O'Malley Folklore Collection Notebooks, Boxes 1–3, National Folklore Collection, UCD.

8   EOM Papers AlA060, Series X, Notebooks, Box 12, Folder 20 and Box 13, Folder 13.

9   EOM Papers AlA060, Series l, Box 1, Folder 15.

Chapter one

1   This tale is from NFC Vol. 4 (pp. 78–80) and was told by Patrick O'Malley on 24 February 1940. Patrick heard this tale from Neenan of Tourmakeedy, County Mayo.

2   This tale is from NFC Vol. 2 (p. 49R) and was told by Patrick O'Malley on 2 February 1940. Daniel was Patsy Mickey's uncle, and this tale happened when Patsy was a young boy and his mother was still alive. Patrick was told this tale by Doctor Burke's sister, who married Domhnall. Fr Leo Richard Ward's (1893–1984) book, *God in an Irish Kitchen* was published in 1939 in the USA.

3   This tale is from NFC Vol. 5 (pp. 73–5) and was told by Jamsie Jordan on 29 February 1940. Jamsie was over two years old when this tale happened in 1869. Dónall drowned in Newport in November 1870.

4   This tale is from NFC Vol. 3 (p. 81) and was told by James O'Malley on 7 February 1940.

5   This tale is from NFC Vol. 3 (p. 97R) and was told by Mickey O'Malley on 8 February 1940. Mickey remembered an old lady telling him this tale.

6   This tale is from NFC Vol. 3 (p. 98R) and was told by John O'Toole on 8 February 1940. There are other tales where the fairies were upset by the activities of humans such as digging into mounds, clearing land, building a house or a graveyard in the 'wrong' place. There was no title for this tale other than 'Tullabaun'.

7   This tale is from NFC Vol. 3 (p. 100L) and was told by Mickey O'Malley on 8 February 1940. Mickey was told this tale by his

mother. Many other people also had this tale. Pat Sammon lived beside Mickey, and he died at eighty-four years in 1915. Pat had seen the battle himself.

8   This tale is from NFC Vol. 3 (p. 109R) and was told by John O'Toole on 10 February 1940. John's father-in-law told him this tale. Crupá is a chronic phosphorous deficiency in cattle known as hypophosphataemia.

9   This tale is from NFC Vol. 3 (p. 102L) and was told by Mickey O'Malley on 8 February 1940.

10 This tale is from NFC Vol. 4 (pp. 1–3) and was told by Jamsie Charlie O'Toole on 9 February 1940. Jamsie got this story from his mother, Nellie Coyne Jordan. It had been handed down by a MacNamara man married to an Inishturk woman. Jamsie's grandmother was a Lavelle who died aged one hundred and four years, and her mother was an O'Malley who told this tale to her when she was ninety-four.

11 This tale is from NFC Vol. 4 (pp. 6–7) and was told by Jamsie Charlie O'Toole on 9 February 1940. Jamsie had seen the woman in about 1890 and knew her for about twenty years. She lived 'til she was about eighty years of age. Jamsie's father was a friend of hers. Jamsie's grandmother, Kathy Lavelle, told him this tale, and she lived 'til 1880.

12 This tale is from NFC Vol. 4 (p. 31) and was told by William O'Malley on 9 February 1940. William heard this tale from both of his grandparents.

13 This tale is from NFC Vol. 4 (p. 48) and was told by William O'Malley on 9 February 1940.

14 This tale is from NFC Vol. 4 (pp. 82–3) and was told by Patrick O'Malley on 24 February 1940. Patrick got this tale from old Patsy Nicholson, who was a shopkeeper in Bunowen, Louisburgh. A spailpín refers to a wandering labourer while a pavee was one from the traveller community.

15   This tale is from NFC Vol. 5 (pp. 20–1) and was told by Jamsie Jordan on 23 February 1940. Jamsie got this tale from Austin Quinn.

16   This tale is from Vol. 5 (pp. 25–7) and was told by Jamsie Jordan on 23 February 1940.

17   This tale is from NFC Vol. 5 (pp. 27–9) and was told by Jamsie Jordan on 23 February 1940. Jamsie got this tale from his mother, and it was from about the 1840s. She was eighty-three when she died in 1924, the youngest of the family. Jamsie's mother's grandfather was Padraic Nolan. Collanmore is sometime called Collan for short.

18   This tale is from NFC Vol. 5 (pp. 34–6) and was told by Tom O'Brien on 28 February 1940. The expression 'overboard' suggests that the child had gone over or died. Mrs Costello, a granddaughter of the old midwife, Maire Gavin, was still living in Carrowmore, outside Newport on the Westport road, in 1940.

19   This tale is from NFC Vol. 5 (pp. 39–41) and was told by Tom O'Brien on 28 February 1940.

20   This tale is from NFC Vol. 5 (pp. 42–3) and was told by Tom O'Brien on 28 February 1940.

21   This tale is from NFC Vol. 5 (p. 41) and was told by Tom O'Brien on 28 February 1940. The mound would have been a fairy mound which was being disturbed by the man's digging.

22   This tale is from Vol. 3 (pp. 25–6) and was told by Patrick O'Malley on 2 February 1940. Archbishop John MacHale (1791–1881) was from Tubbernavine, in Addergoole, near Lough Conn, and his seat was in Tuam. MacHale was an Irish speaker, perceived to be a nationalist, which was unusual for a cleric who had gone to Patrick Stanton's Classical School in Castlebar.

23   This tale is from NFC Vol. 5 (pp. 71–3) and was told by Jamsie Jordan on 29 February 1940.

24   This tale is from NFC Vol. 9 (pp. 81–2) and was told by Patrick Quinn on 24 March 1940.

25   This tale is from NFC Vol. 9 (p. 103) and was told by Patrick Quinn on 4 April 1942. Patrick got this tale from Mrs Regan, who also lived on Inishcottle and who knew the woman in the tale. This tale was also titled 'The woman that gave suck to the fairy child'.

26   This tale is from NFC Vol. 5 (pp. 30–2) and was told by Jamsie Jordan on 23 February 1940. Jamsie was told this tale by his first cousin, James Jordan. Johnny Walsh was forty-four years married when he died in early January 1940. This event took place in 1910. A perch was a place where a light was hung to mark the shipping channel.

27   This tale is from NFC Vol. 5 (pp. 46–7) and was told by Tom O'Brien on 28 February 1940.

28   This tale is from NFC Vol. 5 (p. 48) and was told by Tom O'Brien on 28 February 1940. Tom noted that it is often said that it is bad luck to kill a swan.

29   This tale is from NFC Vol. 2 (p. 60) and was told by Patrick O'Malley on 2 February 1940. Inishclara is the old Irish name for Clare Island.

Chapter two

1   This tale from about 1810 is from NFC Vol. 3 (pp. 38–41) and was told by Jamsie Jordan on 3 February 1940. Paddy Quinn's brother from Inishnakillew was Jamsie's great-grandfather, and he died in 1890 at age eighty. Jamsie reports that Paddy 'was a good careful man in a boat and would never sleep in his boat'. This Paddy Quinn is not related to the Quinns of Inishcottle. Collan refers to the island of Collanmore.

2   This tale is from NFC Vol. 3 (pp. 41–3) and was told by Jamsie Jordan on 3 February 1940. This event occurred in about September 1923. Austin Quinn was also referred to as Alfie in the tale. Jamsie told this tale again on 24 March 1940 and that can be found in Vol. 9 (98–102)

under the title 'The Nets the Fairies Moved'. They are quite similar. According to the later tale, Austin Quinn, Patrick Quinn and Jamsie's cousin, Willie Jordan, were the four men involved.

3   This tale is from NFC Vol. 3 (pp. 43–4) and was told by Jamsie Jordan on 3 February 1940. Rosstoohy is located on a headland near Newport.

4   This tale is from NFC Vol. 3 (pp. 45–6) and was told by Jamsie Jordan on 3 February 1940. Jamsie remembered this event from September 1916. The fire on a boat was usually placed in a small pot resting on the beam seat so that the wind would not get at it. Sand and muck were put around its base. Fire was always brought out in the boats in the autumn season.

5   This tale is from NFC Vol. 10 (pp. 3–5) and was told by Jamsie Jordan on 26 April 1942. The Gallagher brothers sailed to Westport in about 1902.

6   This tale is from NFC Vol. 3 (p. 115L/R) and was told by John O'Toole on 10 February 1940. John heard the tale from Stephen Mullin of Aughris in about 1895, and it related to a fishing incident in about 1860 between Inishshark and Inishbofin. Inishbofin is locally referred to as Bofin and Inishshark as Shark.

7   This tale is from NFC Vol. 3 (p. 47) and was told by Jamsie Jordan on 3 February 1940. The tale was originally told by Pat Quinn, the father of John Quinn of Inishnakillew, and he told it to Jamsie. The flails were two sticks, four feet long and tied together and were used to thresh wheat. The tale comes from about one hundred years before or about 1840. Inishbollog is just to the north of Inishnakillew and Inishcottle.

8   This tale is from NFC Vol. 3 (pp. 50–1) and was told by John Quinn on 3 February 1940. John often heard the tale told by his grandfather, Michael Quinn.

9   This tale is from NFC Vol. 8 (pp. 64–5) and was told by John Geraghty on 16 March 1940. John heard this tale from Mrs Gil Burke, a Gibbons

woman, who lived in Louisburgh after 1850, and she died there soon before 1900. The fisherman was born in about 1880, and some of his children lived on Clare Island.

10   This tale is from NFC Vol. 4 (pp. 24–5) and was told by Jamsie Charlie O'Toole on 9 February 1940. The tragedy occurred on 28 December 1883.

11   This tale is from NFC Vol. 4 (p. 57) and was told by John O'Toole on 9 February 1940. It is a slightly different version from the tale told by Jamsie Charlie O'Toole in the earlier version above. In all, six men drowned on 28 December 1883: Anthony O'Malley and his brother, Michael, who were trying to forestall the seizure of part of their cattle by marking them as if they were McHale cattle belonging to his father-in-law; a McHale who was their brother-in-law; Tony O'Malley, a nephew of the O'Malleys; a herder boy named Moran. Another man, Michael O'Toole, was part of the group, but he couldn't find his stockings that morning and missed the boat.

12   This tale is from NFC Vol. 10 (pp. 20–2) and was told by Jamsie Jordan on 17 May 1942. Jamsie heard this tale from Mickey Kane of Ballure, and it happened in about 1890.

13   This tale is from NFC Vol. 10 (pp. 21–2) and was told by Jamsie Jordan on 17 May 1942. Jamsie heard this tale from his mother, Ellen Coyne Jordan, and others. His mother said Mrs Tom Purcell was a cousin of Jamsie's uncle's wife, and the event took place in about 1860.

14   This tale is from NFC Vol. 5 (pp. 17–18) and was told by Jamsie Jordan on 23 February 1940.

15   This tale is from NFC Vol. 5 (pp. 18–19) and was told by Jamsie Jordan on 23 February 1940. James heard this tale from a sailor who was on board the schooner.

16   This tale is from NFC Vol. 3 (p. 99L/R) and was told by Mickey O'Malley on 8 February 1940. Mickey was told this tale by an old man who died in 1902, when he was eighty-four years.

17 This tale is from NFC Vol. 3 (p. 54) and was told by Jamsie Jordan on 3 February 1940. Jamsie heard the tale from his uncle, John Jordan of Inishnakillew.

18 This tale is from NFC Vol. 9 (pp. 90–2) and was told by Jamsie Jordan on 24 March 1940. Jamsie got this tale from Austin Quinn of Inishnakillew in about 1900.

Chapter three

1 This tale is from NFC Vol. 3 (pp. 16–19) and was told by Patrick O'Malley on 2 February 1940. The original tale was told in rhyme to Patrick by Paddy Geraghty when Patrick was a little ladeen. The tale was also titled 'The Fight to Save Ireland'.

2 This is a possible attempt at 'Corann ins an cor agus camadh is an cam'. The translation provided is O'Malley's original.

3 This tale is from NFC Vol. 8 (pp. 94–7) and was told by Jamsie Jordan on 26 April 1942.

4 This tale is from NFC Vol. 8 (pp. 54–7) and was told by William O'Malley on 15 March 1940.

5 This tale is from NFC Vol. 8 (pp. 57–61) and was told by William O'Malley on 15 March 1940.

6 This tale is from NFC Vol. 8 (pp. 97–8) and was told by Jamsie Jordan on 26 April 1942.

7 This tale is from NFC Vol. 4 (pp. 86–7) and was told by Patrick O'Malley on 24 February 1940. Lord Waterford's family name is Beresford and comes from Cavan.

8 This tale is from AIA Vol. 6 (pp. 30–7) and was told by William O'Malley in early 1940.

Chapter four

1   This tale is from NFC Vol. 4 (pp. 64–5) and was told by Patrick O'Malley on 12 February 1940.

2   This tale is from NFC Vol. 10 (pp. 14–16) and was told by Jamsie Jordan on 17 May 1942.

3   This tale is from NFC Vol. 3 (pp. 23–4) and was told by Patrick O'Malley on 2 February 1940. Patrick got this tale from his mother and her sister who were from Killeen in the far west of Louisburgh. This tale was also called 'The Blind Girl Sees'.

4   This tale is from NFC Vol. 3 (pp. 102R–103) and was told by Mickey O'Malley on 8 February 1940. Mickey was told this tale by his mother, and he remembered that old people around there used to tell it to him also.

5   This tale is from NFC Vol. 5 (pp. 23–5) and was told by Jamsie Jordan on 23 February 1940. Jamsie heard this tale from Johnny Mulhearn himself in about 1895, when Johnny was about sixty-five years old. The incident happened when Johnny was a young man. Durrycoosh is located on the Kilmeena side of Castlebar about a half mile on the Kilmeena side of the Raheen's post office.

6   This tale is from AIA Vol. 6 (pp. 3–12) and was told by William O'Malley in early 1940. William heard this tale in Derrygarrow from Mrs Mary O'Malley, a Gibbons woman. This tale is an International Tale: 330.

7   This tale is from AIA Vol. 6 (pp. 14–15) and was told by William O'Malley in early 1940. William got this tale from his grandmother, Nelly or Ellen Ó Máille. One hundredweight is about 152 kilos or 336 pounds.

Chapter five

1   This tale is from NFC Vol. 8 (p. 2) and was told by John O'Malley on 14 March 1940.

2   This tale is from NFC Vol. 3 (p. 21) and was told by Patrick O'Malley in early 1940. Caher is just south of Louisburgh.

3   This tale is from NFC Vol. 2 (p. 59) and was told by Patrick O'Malley on 2 February 1940. Transportation to Australia was a common punishment.

4   This tale is from NFC Vol. 3 (p. 20) and was told by Patrick O'Malley on 2 February 1940.

5   This tale is from NFC Vol. 4 (p. 34) and was told by William O'Malley on 9 February 1940. The events in this tale are from about 1840.

6   This tale is from AIA Vol. 6 (pp. 40–5) and was told by Mickey O'Malley in early 1940. Mickey was told this tale by an old man named Salmon, which is a common name in Carrowmore. Salmon had heard it from his mother, and she was living at the time of the event in 1820 and knew Edward Lavelle's parents.

7   This tale is from NFC Vol. 5 (pp. 83L–88) and was told by John Quinn on 5 March 1940. J.M. Synge used part of the James Lynchehaun (1858–1946) character as one of the bases for his 'playboy' character in *Playboy of the Western World*. This tale took place in Achill in the 1890s.

8   This tale is from NFC Vol. 3 (pp. 77–8) and was told by James O'Malley on 6 February 1940.

9   This tale is from NFC Vol. 5 (pp. 21–3) and was told by Patrick Quinn on 23 February 1940. Patrick was often told this tale by Austin Quinn of Innishcottle. Breaghwy, near Castlebar, is known locally as Breaffy.

10 This tale is from NFC Vol. 3 (pp. 13–15) and was told by Patrick O'Malley on 2 February 1940. Patrick heard this tale from Patsy Nicholson, William Nicholson's grandson. John Denis Browne later

became the first Marquis of Sligo after the Act of Union of the United Kingdom and Ireland of 1800.

11   This tale is from NFC Vol. 5 (pp. 56–8) and was told by Tom O'Brien on 28 February 1940. Note: '98 refers to the 1798 French invasion in Killala, just north of Ballina and the time of the general rebellion in Ireland in 1798.

12   This poem is from NFC Vol. 3 (88R). No storyteller is clearly identified, but James O'Malley told several of the immediately preceding tales on 7 February 1940. 'Rory of the Hill' is an old reference to the men who fought for Irish freedom over the years or the rebels. 'Blackhead' sheep or 'canny Scotch' and the 'kyloe' cattle were introduced to the west of Ireland from the western Highlands after the Famine. The Gladstone Bill probably refers to the Government of Ireland Bill of 1886 which William Gladstone, MP introduced as prime minister and is often known as the First Home Rule Bill. 'Billy' refers to a loyalist and 'his billy' refers to his dog.

13   This tale is from NFC Vol. 3 (pp. 63–6) and was told by Jamsie Jordan on 3 February 1940. Jamsie remembered James McDonnell coming to their family home on Inishnakillew and putting a lock on the door in 1876 when he was about ten years old. His father, William, had died the year before. His mother and her five children were evicted in 1876.

14   This tale is from NFC Vol. 5 (pp. 59–61) and was told by Tom O'Brien on 28 February 1940.

15   This tale is from NFC Vol. 5 (p. 61) and was told by Tom O'Brien on 28 February 1940. Mr Bingham was Lord Lucan of Castlebar.

16   This tale is from NFC Vol. 4 (p. 70L) and was told by Mickey Gavin on 12 February 1940. Mickey's grandfather on his mother's side was Pat O'Malley. George Charles Bingham, 3rd Earl, Lord Lucan (1810–1877) lost the election in 1857 but was successful in 1865.

17   This tale is from NFC Vol. 4 (p. 69L) and was told by Patrick O'Malley on 24 February 1940.

18 This tale is from NFC Vol. 3 (p. 55) and was told by Jamsie Jordan on 3 February 1940. Buckfield Bridge is off the Newport–Westport road in Kilmeena.

19 This tale is from NFC Vol. 4 (pp. 26–7) and was told by William O'Malley on 9 February 1940. William was told this tale by Mrs Scanlon.

20 This tale is from NFC Vol. 3 (pp. 97R–98L) and was told by Mickey O'Malley on 8 February 1940. A jumper is someone who changed religions in order to get food.

21 This tale is from NFC Vol. 3 (p. 106R) and was told by John O'Toole on 10 February 1940. The Achill Mission or Colony at Dugort, referred to in this tale as the Bird's Nest, was founded by the Church of Ireland Reverend Edward Nangle from County Meath in 1831 as a Protestant proselytising mission and ultimately included a school, cottages, orphanage, hospital and hotel. It declined in the 1880s after Rev. Nangle died in 1883.

22 This tale is from NFC Vol. 4 (pp. 20–2) and was told by Jamsie Charlie O'Toole on 9 February 1940. A process server is a person who is paid to serve an official court notice or 'process' on a tenant.

23 This tale is in NFC Vol. 4 (p. 67L) and was told by Patrick O'Malley on 24 February 1940.

24 This tale is from NFC Vol. 4 (p. 22R) and was told by Jamsie Charlie O'Toole on 9 February 1940. Billy's Pound was located near the quay on Clare Island.

25 This tale is from NFC Vol. 4 (p. 41) and was told by William O'Malley on 9 February 1940. Cloona is just outside Westport. Over the years the landlords for Clare Island included Sir Samuel O'Malley of Roscahill and Kilboyne, his successor the Law Life Insurance Company, Lord Lucan of Castlebar, Thomas McDonnell of Clonna, McDonnell's daughters and finally in 1895, the Congested Districts Board.

26 This tale from the 1850s is from NFC Vol. 3 (pp. 61R–2) and was told by Jamsie Jordan on 3 February 1940. Jordan's grandmother, Maire Máille, Máire Howl (Hughey), had lived in that house with her five

children after her husband died. Luckily, she was able to pay two years' rent, as required. All the other men and their families had to leave Inishnakillew. Jamsie's great-grandfather had seven sons, and his grandfather had five sons.

27   This tale is from NFC Vol. 9 (pp. 1–5) and was told by Tom O'Brien on 17 March 1940. Tom heard this tale from an old man near Moyna Chapel in Kilmeena in about 1910. In the following tale the Lavelles appear as the foreigners fighting the O'Malleys but in this, it is the Danes who are the foreigners fighting the O'Malleys.

28   This tale is from NFC Vol. 3 (pp. 68–70) and was told by James O'Malley on 6 February 1940. In this tale the Lavelles are the foreigners fighting the Ó Máilles and in the preceding tale, it is the Danes who are the foreigners.

29   This tale is from NFC Vol. 5 (pp. 1–3) and was told by Jamsie Jordan on 23 February 1940. Kearns would have left the island in the early 1860s.

30   This tale is from NFC Vol. 8 (pp. 83–4) and was told by Jamsie Jordan on 26 April 1940.

31   This tale is from NFC Vol. 3 (pp. 112–13) and was told by John O'Toole on 10 February 1940. John heard this tale from a grandson of Capt. Coney. Johnny Gibbons was known as an outlaw for his illegal importing and selling of goods on which he paid no taxes.

32   This tale is from NFC Vol. 5 (p. 88) and was told by John Quinn on 5 March 1940. John often heard this tale from his father, but he never heard the Fenian leader's name. The village of Breaghwy is referred to locally as Breaffy.

33   This tale is from NFC Vol. 8 (p. 8) and was told by John O'Malley on 14 March 1940.

34   This tale is from NFC Vol. 5 (pp. 11–13) and was told by Jamsie Jordan on 23 February 1940. The expression 'five-eighths' refers to the lesser people or the commoners. There was no title given to this tale in the notebook.

35   This tale is from NFC Vol. 7 (pp. 16-19) and was told by Tom O'Brien on 3 March 1940. RIC stands for Royal Irish Constabulary.

36   This tale is from NFC Vol. 5 (pp. 51-2) and was told by Tom O'Brien on 28 February 1940. The title 'The Kellys of Cornfield in East Mayo' is also mentioned in the notebook.

37   This tale is from NFC Vol. 4 (pp. 4-5) and was told by Jamsie Charlie O'Toole on 9 February 1940. Jamsie heard this tale from a Farley man when he was one hundred and ten years old, living on Inishturk. He died at one hundred and fourteen years. Farley's father lived 'til he was one hundred and four years and had seen the two men, O'Toole and O'Lorcan.

Chapter six

1   This tale is from NFC Vol. 4 (pp. 30-1) and was told by William O'Malley on 9 February 1940. William was told this tale by two of his grandparents.

2   This tale is from NFC Vol. 5 (pp. 7-11) and was told by Jamsie Jordan on 23 February 1940. Jamsie's father's mother, who lived on Inishnakillew, was a Máille. She was called Máille Hugh. The Hugh Máille name ran in the Jordan family. Jamsie's father died early in 1869 and so Ellen Coyne Jordan was widowed early.

3   This tale is from NFC Vol. 5 (pp. 38-9) and was told by Tom O'Brien on 28 February 1940.

4   This tale is from AIA Vol. 6 (pp. 1-3) and was told by William O'Malley in early 1940. William got this tale from his grandmother, and the events took place in her house in Shannacloy, known as the old stony village.

5   This tale is from NFC Vol. 7 (pp. 76R-77) and was told by Mickey Gavin on 14 March 1940. Geraghty worked in Aillemore and died in about 1890. His father wasn't from Aillemore, but his wife was from Bundorragha, near the Killaries.

6   This tale is from NFC Vol. 8 (p. 79) and was told by Patrick Quinn on 26 April 1942.

7   This tale is from NFC Vol. 9 (p. 83) and was told by Jamsie Jordan on 24 March 1940. The house in this tale was owned by Jamsie's mother's sister, his aunt and uncle, and the tale was from about 1840.

8   This tale is from NFC Vol. 9 (pp. 95–7) and was told by Jamsie Jordan on 24 March 1942. Jamsie got this tale from Walter Máille of Inishnakillew in about 1890.

9   This tale is from NFC Vol. 9 (p. 88) and was told by Jamsie Jordan on 24 March 1940. An féar gorta (the hungry grass) refers to a phenomenon whereby someone is overcome with a sudden, insatiable hunger after walking on a patch or type of supernatural grass. Jamsie's father, William Jordan, was married to his mother, Ellen Coyne, at the time of this tale.

10 This tale is from AIA Vol. 6 (p. 40) and was told by Mickey O'Malley in early 1940.

11 This tale is from NFC Vol. 4 (p. 23) and was told by Jamsie Charlie O'Toole on 8 February 1940. Fr Quinn was from near Castlebar and died in about 1932. John McEvilly (1818–1902) was born in Louisburgh and was Archbishop of Tuam, 1881–1902.

12 This tale is from NFC Vol. 5 (pp. 36–7) and was told by Tom O'Brien on 28 February 1940.

13 This tale is from NFC Vol. 4 (pp. 61–2) and was told by Patrick O'Malley on 12 February 1940.

Afterword

1   Thomas Johnson Westropp, 'A Study of the Folklore on the Coast of Connacht, Ireland', *Folklore*, Dec. 30, 1918, Vol. 29, No. 4, 305.

2   Delargy, J.H., *The Gaelic Story-teller With Some Notes on Gaelic Folk-tales* (London: Geoffrey Cumberlege, 1945), p. 46.

3 Autobiographical Statement, Ernie O'Malley Papers, New York University Library, Archives of Irish America #060 (hereafter 'EOM Papers AIA060'), Series I, Box 1, Folder 7. See also in Cormac O'Malley and Nicholas Allen (eds), *Broken Landscapes: Selected Letters of Ernie O'Malley, 1924–1957* (Dublin: Lilliput Press, 2011), p. 223.

4 Eve Morrison in S. Aiken et al. (eds), *The Men Will Talk to Me: Ernie O'Malley's Interviews with the Northern Divisions* (Dublin: Merrion Press, 2018), p. 245.

5 Ernie O'Malley to Eithne Golden, 7 March 1940. EOM Papers AIA060, Series III, Box 5, Folder 4; see also in O'Malley and Allen, *Broken Landscapes*, p. 185.

6 Ibid.

7 Ernie O'Malley, *On Another Man's Wound* (Cork: Mercier Press, 2013), p. 135.

8 O'Malley to Golden, 7 March 1940.

9 Diarmuid Ó Giolláin, 'An Béaloideas agus an Stáit', *Béaloideas*, 1989, Vol. 57, p. 163.

10 David Lloyd, 'Afterword on Republican Reading', in O'Malley and Allen, *Broken Landscapes*, pp. 382–3.

11 Bo Almqvist, 'The Irish Folklore Commission: Achievement and Legacy', *Béaloideas*, 1977–1979, Vol. 45–47, p. 12.

12 O'Malley, *On Another Man's Wound*, p. 27.

13 Ibid, pp. 106–7, 138.

14 For a broader discussion, see Benjamin Ragan, 'Ghosts, haunted houses, spooky pigs and the War of Independence', *RTÉ Brainstorm*, 21 April 2022.

15 Witness Statement of Andrew McDonnell, Bureau of Military History Witness Statement (BMH WS) No. 1768, p. 37.

16 Witness Statement of Ailbhe Ó Monacháin, BMH WS No. 298, pp. 40–1.

17 Witness Statement of Martin Conneely, BMH WS No. 1611, p. 19.

18 See 'The Man That Didn't Know Where He Was' (p. 35); An Féar Gorta (p. 180); An Féar Gorta on the Roads (p. 181).

19 Dáithí Ó hÓgáin, *Irish Superstitions: Irish Spells, Old Wives' Tales and Folk Beliefs* (Dublin: Gill & MacMillan Ltd, 2002), pp. 60-1.

20 'The Poor Boy That Became a Doctor', (p. 112).

21 'Sir Neal O'Donel of Newport Helps Kilmeena Men', (p. 134).

22 Of the twenty-six informants included in O'Malley's fieldwork, three were women ('Mrs P.J. Kelly', 'Mrs Micky O'Malley' and 'Mrs Geraghty'). However, the women's materials were either untranscribable or insufficient in content for inclusion in the present volume.

23 Mícheál Briody, *The Irish Folklore Commission 1935–1970: History, Ideology, Methodology* (Helsinki: Studia Fennica, 2016), p. 58.

24 'The Woman That Buried Her Brother', Ernie O'Malley Folklore Collection Notebooks, NFC (UCD), NFC Vol. 4 (p. 60R).

25 'Eviction of Ellen Coyne Jordan', (p. 126).

26 Guy Beiner, *Remembering the Year of the French: Irish Folk History and Social Memory* (Madison: The University of Wisconsin Press, 2007), p. 12.

27 For a comprehensive study of Protestants in the twentieth-century Irish folk tradition, see Deirdre Nuttall, *Different and the Same: A Folk History of the Protestants of Independent Ireland* (Dublin: Eastwood Books, 2020).

28 For O'Malley's unpublished short story, entitled 'Admirals for a Day', see EOM Papers NYUL AIA060, Series 1, Box 1, Folder 4.

29 *OAMW*, p. 133.

30 Ernie O'Malley to Eithne Golden Sax, 10 July 1955, EOM Papers AIA060, Series III, Box 5, Folder 4; see also *Broken Landscapes*, p. 340.

Index

Achill Island, xiv, 4, 47, 48, 51, 54,
  113, 114, 116, 138, 139, 164, 183,
  191, 207
Almqvist, Bo, 192
America; see also Emigration;
  O'Malley's time in, xviii, 191;
  References to within oral
  tradition, 4, 5, 111, 112, 115, 152,
  153, 156, 191; Local migration
  link to Cleveland, Ohio, 116,
  183, 191; American cultural
  influences, 192

Bairéad, Ciarán, xiv

Castlebar, 114, 119, 123, 131–133, 137,
  145, 155 ; O'Malley's childhood
  in, xvii,

Clare Island, 38, 52, 53–56, 139–143,
  149, 152, 182, 195, 207
Congested District Board, 54,
  143–144, 162
Cromwell, Oliver, xiv, 162–163
Cú Chulainn, xviii, 192

Devil; lore relating to, 19, 92–93,
  94–101
Doolough, 136

Emigration, 4, 5, 111–112, 139–140,
  152, 156, 183, 190, 191; returned
  emigrants, 5, 159–160, 183, 191;
  to England/Scotland, 16, 22, 24,
  38, 59, 111, 117, 124, 147, 169
Eviction, 1, 126–128, 133, 136, 145,
  162, 195

mac Cumhaill, Fionn, xvii, 192; in
collected lore, 67–69
Mac Lochlainn, Brian, xiv
Medicine; local healers, 169–172,
175–176
Meyer, Kuno, xviii

New Mexico, xviii
Newport, Kilmeena, 5, 45, 92,
113–116, 122, 134, 159, 178–180,
183, 214, 218; O'Malley home
at Burrishoole.Lodge, xix,
190

Ó Duilearga, Séamus, xiii, xix, 189,
190
O'Malley (or ÓMáille) family lore,
146–151
Ó Moghráin, Pádraig, xiv
On Another Man's Wound, xvii, xix,
191
Ó Súilleabháin, Seán, 190

Rebellion; see also Fenianism;
1798, xiv, 117–125, 196, 223
Religion; participation of the
clergy in affairs/politics, 17–18,

56, 58, 87–88, 92–93, 101, 105–
106, 117–118, 129–130, 142–144,
156–157, 176–177, 182–183;
sacred places, 5–6, 182–183;
conversion, 88–89; 137–139;
jumpers, 137–139, burials, 7–8
Roscahill, 23, 32–33, 126, 158,
177–178, 224

Saint Martin, 91–92
Saint Patrick, 5–6, 88–90
Sea: boats; 59, 60–62; drowning,
32–35, 48–49, 53–61
Seals, 50–53

Trials/disputes, 78, 108–110,
114–116, 155–156
Toor, Frances, xviii

Westport area, 9, 26–29, 33–38,
47, 54, 58–59, 88, 123, 128–131,
133, 135, 139, 141–142, 146, 152,
157–162, 169–173, 183
Westropp, Thomas Johnson,
189–190, 197

Young, Ella, xviii, 213